I·SAW T̤H̤E̤ LORD

A Pilgrimage Through Isaiah 6

I·SAW THE LORD

A Pilgrimage Through Isaiah 6

• by •

Kenneth L. Waters Sr.

UPPER ROOM BOOKS
NASHVILLE

I SAW THE LORD: A PILGRIMAGE THROUGH ISAIAH 6

Cover Art Interpretation on page 111.

Cover Design: Sheila R. Williams
Interior Design and Layout: Nancy Cole
First Printing: October 1996 (3)

Library of Congress Cataloging-in-Publication Data

Waters, Kenneth L., Sr. 1953-
    I saw the Lord : a pilgrimage through Isaiah 6 / Kenneth L. Waters Sr.
        p.   cm.
        ISBN 0-8358-0784-3 (pbk.)
    1. Bible. O.T. Isaiah VI—Criticism, interpretation, etc.
    2. Prophets—Calling of—Biblical teaching. 3. Vocation—Biblical teaching. 4. Isaiah (Biblical prophet) 5. Spiritual life—Biblical teaching. 6. Afro-Americans—Religion.
    I. Title.
    BS1515.2.W36 1996
    224'.106—dc20   96-5062
                                                              CIP

Printed in the United States of America

To Michael W. Waters,
my oldest son,
for whom I thank God
and of whom I am very proud.

• *Table of Contents* •

· *Acknowledgments* ·

I wish to acknowledge with deep appreciation my wonderful wife, Justine Bell Waters, Ph.D., Professor of Public Administration at California State University, Dominguez Hills, for her unfaltering support and encouragement in the composing of this book. I thank her particularly for lending her considerable data-processing skills to the preparation of the original manuscript. Her thoroughgoing love for me and steadfast commitment to my whole ministry makes her a living testament of God's grace in my life.

I would not miss this opportunity to express gratitude for the loving support of my family: my father, Ollie James Waters; mother, Marie Porter Waters; elder brother, David James Waters; younger brother, Don Waters; sister-in-law, Zerrie Waters; sister, Brenda Marie Waters; mother-in-law, Ida Bell; sons, Joseph Grant, Craig Zackery, Michael, Gregory Bell, Kenneth L. Jr.; and brother-in-law James Bell Jr. I am thankful also for the legacy and memory of my father-in-law, James A. Bell Sr.

I wish also to acknowledge the camaraderie and support of my fellows in the African American Writers Workshop of the General Board of Discipleship of the United Methodist Church: Abena Safiyah Fosua (formerly Andrea Bishop), Anthony Alexander, Deborah Atwater,* Valerie Banks, Cordella Brown, Steve Duncan, Gwendolyn Ebron,* Janice Frederick-Watts, Robert Gardner, Michael Harriot,* Janette Hightower, Kwasi Issa Kena (formerly Thomas Bishop), Cynthia Hopson, Elaine Jenkins, Sebrena Lewis, Mary Miller, Lynn Mims, Byron Robertson, Lillian Smith, Lloyd Terrell, Odell Thompson, and Jerry Ruth Williams.

I express appreciation also for General Board of Discipleship staff for their investment of time, interest, and energy in our development as writers: Helen Bell, Cheryl Capshaw,* Marigene Chamberlain, Craig Gallaway, Lynn Gilliam,* George Graham, Janice Grana, Terrence Hayes, David Hazlewood, Jan Knight,

Carol Krau, Marilyn Magee, JoAnn Miller, John Mogabgab, Victor Perez-Silvestry, Mary Lou Redding, David White, and Karen F. Williams.

Those names marked with asterisks were members of my process group, the first to hear the proposal for this book and provide valuable feedback.

I am thankful also for New Testament and Old Testament faculty of the Fuller Theological Seminary for insights that I have learned there as a Ph.D. student in New Testament. They, however, are not responsible for any errors contained in this book.

I deeply appreciate the commitment of the editors of Upper Room Books to this work, and I am grateful for the relationship I was able to cultivate with many of them at the Writers' Workshop.

Any deficiency remaining in these pages is certainly mine alone.

Finally I express appreciation for the members of the Vermont Square United Methodist Church of Los Angeles, where I am assigned as pastor and with whom I am joined in the exploration of spiritual life.

• *Introduction* •

What does it mean to have a spiritual experience and live a spiritual life? What difference does it make? Why should we seek to be spiritual people? There are other variations of these questions whose shape and form depend upon the religious, social, and cultural context in which they are asked. What does it mean to be saved? converted? born again? regenerated? redeemed? transformed? We hear these terms used in church or in church related situations, but their meanings are not always clear, neither to everyone in the church nor to many outside of the church.

We need an approach to the subject of spiritual renewal that does not presuppose that we know what is meant by the words we frequently use in church. We also need a way of talking about spiritual experience that does not become overly fixated upon only one aspect of the experience. The sixth chapter of Isaiah, a well-known and much beloved passage of the Bible, appears to be an especially attractive foundation for our approach.

While preparing a message for a service of confirmation over fifteen years ago, I was first struck by the richness of Isaiah 6. Usually, this passage is designated the "Call of Isaiah." But in preparing to use the text as the basis of my message, I saw that far more was happening in this text than just the prophet's calling. After some effort at analysis of the text, I discovered that the passage can be neatly arranged into as many as ten phases of Isaiah's experience:

1. Vision (seeing)   6. Cleansing
2. Audition (hearing)   7. Confirmation
3. Sensation (feeling)   8. Calling
4. Conviction   9. Commitment
5. Confession   10. Commission

These ten aspects of spiritual experience constituted Isaiah's encounter with God. I found that a discussion of spirituality within the parameters of each of these ten facets provided a thorough exploration of the meaning of spiritual transformation. Since then I have employed this "Isaiah schema" in small group settings where the discussion focused upon spirituality, and the results have always been good. As a sometime instructor in the Los Angeles District Lay Speaker's School, I have found the ten-fold pattern of Isaiah 6 a most effective way of interpreting the meanings of spirituality and calling to my students.

The premise of this book is that one way to enhance spiritual insight, growth, and development is to talk about these things in class or small group settings. Questions or discussion starters at the end of each chapter and a study leader's guide in the back are designed to facilitate such activity. Of course, it is my prayer that this book will be just as helpful to the individual reader in a private setting.

Each aspect of Isaiah's encounter with the Lord is applied to help us understand the shape, character, and importance of our own spiritual experiences. Illustrations drawn mostly from the author's personal life experiences are offered only to help illuminate the meaning of spiritual life. Names have been changed to honor the privacy of the individuals involved.

Scholarly investigation of the Book of Isaiah and chapter 6 in particular has, of course, generated a staggering amount of debate over issues of authorship, dating, text transmission and composition, Hebrew translation and phraseology, historical background, setting, narrative structure, and interpretation. Open engagement with these issues would have distracted from our main focus upon spirituality; however, awareness of and familiarity with the debate informs our efforts.

If the deep burning question of someone's heart about any aspect of his or her spiritual pilgrimage is finally answered through engagement with this book, then its purpose will have been fulfilled.

I Saw the Lord
• *Vision* •

In the year that King Uzziah died, I saw the LORD sitting on a throne, high and lofty; and the hem of his robe filled the temple. Seraphs were in attendance above him; each had six wings: with two they covered their faces, and with two they covered their feet, and with two they flew.

— Isaiah 6:1-2

Ghost in the Clouds

"Look, Dad, a ghost in the clouds!"

"What?" I said.

At the time we were rolling to a routine stop at the intersection that exits our neighborhood. My ten–year–old son blurted out his intriguing discovery as I prepared to make a left hand turn onto a main thoroughfare.

"There's a ghost in the clouds!" he responded while pointing to my left.

I made a quick glance to my left just before committing our vehicle to a left turn during a break in cross traffic.

"What ghost?" I asked after a glimpse of fluffy white clouds nestling upon the horizon.

Kenneth Jr. could now direct my attention straight ahead to the bank of clouds that inspired his fertile imagination.

"See, there are the eyes and the mouth," he said, pointing to blue spaces appearing through the billowy puffs.

I had only a few moments before making our next turn toward the freeway, but this was sufficient time to share in my son's playful vision. Yes, when I looked at them in a certain way the spaces in the clouds did form the pattern of eyes and a mouth. Imagining the contours of a spectral face emerging from the thick rolling mist became easy.

"Oh, yes," I observed to Kenneth's amusement, "there is a ghost in the clouds."

My youngest son drew out a playful moment from me that day in our automobile as he had done numerous times before. This time, however, he also drew out something worth reflecting upon. In order to see the ghostly face against the backdrop of a floating white mass, I had to coax my eyes to see certain features in the airy nebulae while ignoring others. Something in my mind had to shift into position to receive the new vision that my son and my eyes were offering me; otherwise my son would have pointed to the clouds in vain.

An arresting lesson springs from this light episode in our automobile: seeing God in the midst of our human experience is very much like seeing "a ghost in the clouds." We must focus on certain aspects of our experience while ignoring others, and we must position ourselves inwardly to receive in a new way what our eyes are showing us.

Seeing God requires some effort, but it is effort to perceive a Presence that is really there and wants to be seen. Our challenge is to become more consciously aware of and sensitive to all the big and little ways that God makes God's own Self known to us. Awareness and sensitivity of this type are what we mean by the words "spiritual eyes."

A Real Encounter

Isaiah saw the Lord. He testifies to a real event of seeing God in a particular place during a particular period of time. We learn from Isaiah's account about the character of God and what it means, generally speaking, to see the Lord.

Isaiah speaks as if his vision of the Lord were an actual experience of his physical eyes. He was not dreaming, hallucinating, nor having a flight of the imagination. He actually saw the Lord.

Seeing for physically sighted persons is ordinarily a message conveyed by the optical nerves in the eyes to the visual center of the brain. Seeing is ordinarily achieved by physically unsighted persons through messages conveyed to the brain by any of the other senses. In either case, seeing is primarily a physical act and secondarily, a mental act. Isaiah gives us the impression that his perception of the Lord's being was at least a physical-mental act of this type. That is to say, it was real.

There were other Old Testament human sightings of the Divine Person that were understood as no less real. Moses saw the Lord, first in the form of a burning bush (Exodus 3:1-6) and then as a consuming fire upon the Sinai mountaintop (Exodus 24:17). Moses was finally allowed to see the back of the Lord also on Sinai (Exodus 33:23). Ezekiel saw the Lord in the form of a human being whose torso had the appearance of "gleaming bronze" encased in fire, and who was seated above a throne (Ezekiel 1:26-28, RSV). Daniel saw the Lord in the form of one that was "ancient of days" with raiment "white as snow" and hair like "pure wool" who was also seated upon a throne (Daniel 7:9, RSV).

There were also New Testament human sightings of the Divine Person; however, in the New Testament the revealing of the Divine Self is specifically through the person of Jesus Christ. Particularly notable are the appearances of Jesus to Mary Magdalene and the other women disciples after he was raised from the dead (Matthew 28:8-10; Mark 16:9-11; John 20:11-18).

The eleven remaining men disciples and numerous others also saw the Risen Lord (Matthew 28:16-20; Mark 16:12-20; Luke 24:15, 36-53; John 20:19-29; 21:1-23; 1 Corinthians 15:3-7).

Stephen, the first deacon, in the fleeting moments of his final breath saw the "heavens opened, and the Son of man standing at the right hand of God" (Acts 7:56, RSV).

Saul of Tarsus who became Paul the Apostle saw the Risen Lord in the form of a blinding light on the road to Damascus (Acts 9:3-7; 22:4-16; 26:9-18; Galatians 1:13-17).

John the Revelator saw the Lord in the form of "one like a son of man" with hair like "white wool" and feet like "burnished bronze, refined as in a furnace" (Revelation 1:12-15, RSV).

These biblical persons' experiences were not merely "mystical" meetings that could be explained away in any number of ways. They were real encounters with a real person from the realm of the Divine. Isaiah's testimony would not mean much of anything, especially to the person in the streets, if it was not about a real encounter.

Isaiah, however, saw *the Lord*. This means that even though it was a real experience of seeing, as we ordinarily understand the physical-mental act of visual perception, it had to involve more than an ordinary act of the physical eyes and brain. God is not a physical being inhabiting physical space. God is, therefore, not accessible to the physical senses in the way that other persons and objects are. Something more must be taking place in Isaiah's witness.

Clearly, Isaiah's sighting of the Lord was a spiritual event involving the spiritual eye. Nevertheless, it was an event as real as beholding the face of a beloved friend.

Here we are challenged to overthrow a premise that we have inherited from modern culture, namely, that the perceptions of our physical faculties are real and reliable, while those of our spiritual faculties are not. On the contrary, we declare that what we see with our spiritual eyes is just as real as what we see with our physical eyes. But how can we say this?

We can say this after we first consider what the word "real" means. Something is real when it has independent existence apart from our perception of it or lack thereof. When we finally come to know about it, whatever it is, our common sense tells us that it just did not come into being when we learned about it. It existed before. The realm of the spirit or the supernatural is like this. The realm of the spirit or the supernatural has independent existence whether we perceive it or not. When we finally come to know about the realm of the spirit or the supernatural, our common sense tells us that this realm has always been there. The question is, "How do we come to know about the realm of the spirit or the supernatural?" That is the question we hope to answer in these pages.

What we call *real* simply cannot be limited to what we see with our physical eyes. There is a reality beyond the physical world. Isaiah caught more than a glimpse of that reality. We, to some extent, can share in Isaiah's vision.

A Timely Event

Several aspects of Isaiah's vision are of crucial importance for our own efforts at seeing the Lord. We begin with the vision's location in time, that is, "In the year that King Uzziah died."

Uzziah (ca.783-742 B.C.E.) became King of Judah at age sixteen by popular acclaim (2 Kings 15:1-2; 2 Chronicles 26:1), and he was a devout seeker of the Lord under the tutelage of Zechariah (2 Chronicles 26:5).[1] He led Judah to a height of prosperity and influence that rivalled the glorious reigns of David and Solomon. Uzziah so distinguished himself as a military genius that his fame spread to the borders of Egypt (2 Chronicles 26:8). The army he organized was particularly formidable by reason of innovative and technologically advanced weaponry such as stone and arrow catapults (2 Chronicles 26:14-15). He was furthermore the architect of a building program to fortify the gates of Jerusalem (2 Chronicles 26:9) and also the designer of an irrigation system that resulted in the mushrooming of agriculture in the Judean wilderness (2 Chronicles 26:10).

Uzziah's story takes a tragic turn when his pride drove him to enter the temple and attempt an offering of incense upon the altar. This would have been a clear trespass upon priestly territory. When Azariah the Priest and his phalanx of eighty priests denied Uzziah access to the altar, the King became

---

[1] Not to be confused with the prophet Zechariah (Zechariah 1:1) who lived about two centuries after Uzziah.

angry. His arrogant outburst brought upon him the affliction of leprosy and, later, a lonely death (2 Chronicles 26:16-21).

It may be that the death of Uzziah was more than a historical reference point for Isaiah's vision of the Lord. It may well have been a catalyst for that vision. Uzziah, while he lived, may have somehow blocked Isaiah's ability to see the Lord. In the African American preaching and teaching tradition the insight that Isaiah could not see the Lord until the departure of Uzziah is a widely held belief. After all, Uzziah was a good King who elicited love, admiration, and respect. One can readily see how Isaiah could have been so enraptured with a vision of Uzziah that he could not see God. Tragically, many persons today are so obsessed with the people they idolize that they cannot see God.

We should not overlook a basic purpose that Isaiah undoubtedly had for speaking of the death of Uzziah: to give us a time frame for his encounter with the Lord. Clearly, for Isaiah, there is no distinction between the encounter with God and spiritual transformation. The death of Uzziah, whatever more it may have been for Isaiah, was at least a milestone or time-marker in Isaiah's spiritual pilgrimage. Referring to it was Isaiah's way of saying "this is when I saw the Lord." This identification of a time frame is important because any real experience we have must be located in time. An encounter with the Lord involves the Divine breaking into our time and space rather than our departure from these boundaries of human existence.

Implications abound from this observation. Since it is God who breaks into our realm rather than we who break into God's realm, a vision of or encounter with God is ultimately the initiative of God. We may seek to see God, but still we can do nothing to achieve this end except eliminating those earthly obsessions that impede our perception of God's presence in our lives; and even this must be done with God's help. We should not seek to "work ourselves" into a vision of God for we cannot. A vision of God is a gift that can only be received with awe and gratitude. Indeed, it is both an awesome thing and a tremendously gracious act whenever Almighty God condescends to enter the creaturely realm.

Isaiah's framing of God's self-disclosure in "the year that King Uzziah died" is nevertheless not as specific as it could be. There is no mention of a month, day, or hour for Isaiah's vision. Indeed, nothing more specific than the year 742 B.C.E. or thereabouts is known about the time of Uzziah's death. A high degree of chronological specificity was not important in Isaiah's testimony. Only that the prophet's sighting of the Divine was an event that occurred in history was important. Those of us who come out of religious traditions that emphasize ability to name "a day and hour" for our first conscious encounter with God may need to inspect this feature of Isaiah's testimony more closely.

We cannot deny that Isaiah's encounter with God, that is to say his spiritual transformation, was rather sudden and dramatic and, therefore, fixed at a specific point in time; but the fact that he did not say more specifically the time this encounter occurred shows that "the day and hour" had no overwhelming importance. Whether we come to know God gradually over a period of years or suddenly in a matter of moments is of fading significance next to the verity that we have come to know God.

High and Lofty

We should now explore Isaiah's testimony more closely. Isaiah saw the Lord robed, seated, and elevated upon a throne that rose high above his head. The Lord's sovereignty and power as King of the Universe is displayed with all dazzling brilliance through the posture of majesty that God assumes in the prophet's vision. God's posture and position convey a crucial message in Isaiah's sighting of the Divine. The posture of "sitting upon a throne" and a position "high and lofty" are declarations of who God is and where God is. Simply stated, God is Sovereign Ruler of the Universe and abides in exalted majesty above all creatures.

Crucial is the vision of who and where God is because it enables us to see who and where we are. Who are we? Where are we? We are creatures of the Sovereign God and we dwell in the creaturely realm. This means that while God dwells in exalted majesty and power, we dwell in weak dependence upon our environment and the One who sustains it.

Indeed, part of what it means to see God (who and where God is) is to see ourselves (who and where we are). As we shall see, when Isaiah saw God, Isaiah also saw himself. Although it seems that Isaiah first saw God and then himself, it is probably better to understand the two perceptions as occurring simultaneously. The vision of God and the vision of self are so closely related that one cannot happen without the other. The achievement of one becomes the achievement of the other. Although there is no first and second order of occurrence in the achievement of the two visions, there can be an order of approach. We can strive to see God by striving to see ourselves first.

Answers now emerge for the questions, "What does it mean to see God?" and "How can we see God?" First, "to see God is to see ourselves." Second, "We can see God by first seeing ourselves." In both cases we mean seeing ourselves as we really are and as we really stand in relationship to God. In this way, what we see when we look at ourselves becomes not a mirror of but a window to God.

The Fullness of God

As Isaiah beheld the enthroned figure of the Divine, even God's regal skirts appeared vibrant with life as they filled the temple with their billowing folds. The temple is suddenly transformed into a microcosm of the universe, while the robe symbolizes God's presence. The message of the robe is that God's presence fills the universe. However, it is only "the hem of his robe" that "filled the temple." This means that while God's presence fills the universe, God's person is not exhausted in the universe. Indeed, that part of God which fills the universe is only as the hem of God's robe. God's independent and separate being abides above and beyond the cosmos with an integrity unique to God, yet God extends the Divine Self into the realm of creation only to the meager extent that creation can contain the Divine Presence.

There are those who purport to see God in creation. Their word has some merit since, "The heavens are telling the glory of God; and the firmament proclaims his handiwork" (Psalm 19:1). Some, however, err in making God coterminous with what they see in creation. There is an aspect of God's being that is separate and removed from God's creation. Indeed, it is the greater aspect of God's being that is separate and removed from creation. We usually refer to this aspect of the Divine Self as God's holiness. Isaiah saw this aspect of God, as we shall see in the pages ahead, but in order to see the holiness of God, Isaiah had to be exposed to God's higher presence, that is, that aspect of God's person that dwells above and beyond the order of created things. How can we experience God's higher presence and see God's holiness? Isaiah did only one thing. He became ready for the experience.

We have already spoken of eliminating from our view the distracting obsessions that impede our vision of God, whether they be people we idolize or other objects that excite our passion. Also we have spoken of the need to see ourselves as we really are and as we really stand in relationship to God. We must now further realize that the world of created things offers us only a partial view of God, creating the need to look beyond nature in order to see God. When we have done these things we have begun to become ready to experience the fullness of God (God's higher presence or God's holiness). But still more is to be done.

Other requirements for experiencing the fullness of God become clear as we continue to explore the vision of Isaiah.

Worshipful and Worthy

Isaiah's sighting of the Divine was not restricted to a vision of God alone. Isaiah saw the seraphs or seraphim hovering above the Lord. These six-winged spirit-creatures had a special function that we shall examine later since this function had to do more with what Isaiah heard than what he saw. Still there is a significance to their very presence and posture in the witness of Isaiah.

Isaiah's encounter with God was actually an encounter with a community. Isaiah saw God in the midst of an untold number of angelic beings, a supernatural society, a celestial community. Furthermore, these angelic beings constituted a worshiping community. Intriguingly, they worshiped with more than the words they proclaimed; with the deployment of their respective six wings and the posture each assumed, each made a nonverbal declaration about the character of God.

With two wings they covered their faces. No creature in heaven, earth, nor beneath the earth is worthy to look upon the majestic countenance of Almighty God, and even more startling, no earthly creature is able to survive the experience of looking upon the Lord (Exodus 33:20). Herein lies the first paradox of Isaiah's experience. He was able to see the Person of God when no other creature could, and furthermore, he lived to tell about it. The paradox, however, can be explained. Isaiah had a genuine encounter with the Divine, but it was still a human experience occurring within the parameters of human limitations. It was still only a vision and not a transportation of Isaiah's being to a higher plane of existence. It was not even the "translation" of human being that John the Apostle promises in his word:

> Beloved, we are God's children now; what we will be has not yet been revealed. What we do know is this: when he is revealed, we will be like him, for we will see him as he is.
>
> — 1 John 3:2

The seraphs from their privileged positions communicated a message to Isaiah concerning what it meant to abide in the presence of God, however, this message itself had to be filtered through the protective envelope of Isaiah's creaturely environment by means of a vision.

With two wings they covered their feet. Here is not only a powerful nonverbal statement about the person of God but also a poignant point of contact with the human being. Covering the feet in a way more acute then covering the face represents the attempt to shield God from the lowest aspects of human character. It is a recognition of our fundamental unworthiness to appear in the presence of God. Irrelevant is the observation that spiritual beings of a higher order such as the seraphs would not share the baseness inherent in the human personality; a baseness, which, in this vision, is symbolized by the angels' feet. It is the message of the gesture that is important. If the angelic beings must cover their feet which never touch the earth, how much more so must we cover ours which have accumulated the dust and grime of earthly sojourn.

Herein lies another paradox. Isaiah must hide the baseness of his personality from the Divine Presence lest he be an affront to God; yet he cannot hide it, and the fact that he cannot becomes crucial for his salvation.

The inability to hide our unworthiness is prerequisite to recognizing our unworthiness; and this in turn, is prerequisite to salvation. Salvation does not mean the removal of all unworthiness. Even the sinless seraphs are yet unworthy to appear in God's presence; but it does mean the recognition and acknowledgment of unworthiness. For Isaiah his recognition and acknowledgment occurred when the seraphs did the same.

With two wings they flew. Some persons may be compelled to understand this deployment of wings as a show of unworthiness to even stand in the presence of God; that is, to share the ground upon which God's throne, let alone the Self of God, stood. This understanding, of course, would not be consistent with God's command to the human Moses: "Come no closer! Remove the sandals from your feet, for the place on which you are standing is holy ground" (Exodus 3:5).

Admittedly, with effort we can find a way to see how Moses' obedient act of sharing the ground with God is consistent with the seraphs' self-abasing avoidance of the ground. We may say, for instance, that it is the soiled sandals of Moses rather than his relatively unsoiled feet that become the symbol of human baseness, and for this reason his sandals had to be put away in the holy presence of God. There is much to commend this reconciliation between Isaiah's experience of God and that of Moses. However, there is still a better understanding of what is meant by the seraphs' hovering flight.

If using their wings to cover their faces and feet was the seraphs' way of identifying with the human, using their wings to fly was their way of identifying with God. They may have thought, *As God dwells above the earth, so do we; as God is unbounded so are we. We are the community of God.*

Again we have a paradox. The community of God is constituted by the angelic host, yet that community is here extended to include the human, namely, Isaiah. The means of inclusion is through worship. It bears emphasis that worship is our means of inclusion in the community of God.

Worship enables us to see God in the fullness of God's holiness. Our vision of God can never be complete without encountering God in the midst of the worshiping community.

Notable in the vision of Isaiah is that God appears as a social, communal, and relational being. God interacts with a social environment, belongs to a community, and relates to creatures. The astonishing feature of this aspect of God's gregarious character is that it embraces the family of humanity also.

Believing Is Seeing

This chapter has been about seeing God; an experience that is just as real as seeing anything else, though with a different set of eyes, spiritual eyes.

Yet, we cannot deny that even the physical eyes can be fooled. Both our eyes and our minds can play tricks on us. How much more likely can we be fooled by our spiritual eyes?

Let us be reminded that there are ways of verifying or testing what we think we see to establish both its degree of reality and the reliability of our physical senses. Spiritual perceptions are usually considered beyond this type of verification or testing, and are therefore dismissed as overwrought imagination. This is a grievous error.

From our exploration of Isaiah's vision of God, we have also established the tests for verifying that our spiritual vision of God is true and reliable. Let us ask ourselves the following questions:

1. Have we removed from our view those objects of obsession that block our view of God?
2. Have we seen ourselves as we really are and as we stand in relation to God?
3. Have we realized how partial a view of God creation offers us, which, in turn, requires us to look beyond?
4. Have we sought the fullness of God in the midst of the worshiping community?

If we have done these things, then we have seen God, and our vision of God is true and reliable.

What Manner of Eyes

I began my pastoral ministry at age eighteen in the backwoods of central Texas when I was a pre-divinity student in Paul Quinn College.

My first Saturday evening as pastor was spent visiting the homes of my new parishioners with my chief steward accompanying me to show me around and introduce me to each church member. Since my church provided no parsonage and I lived in campus housing during the week, I was to spend the night in the home of my chief steward.

The round of visits took all evening since we spent some time in the home of each family. At the last home we visited we stayed for a considerable time after nightfall.

Time came to leave. We said goodbyes on the front porch. The door was shut and the porch light was turned off. Suddenly, I was enveloped in the deepest, blackest night I had ever experienced. There were no stars, no moon, no streetlights, not even fireflies, and we had no flashlight or candle to provide relief from the stifling black of the deep backwoods night. I became frightened. "Mr. Oglesby, I cannot see a thing!" I said desperately appealing to my elderly companion in the midst of impenetrable dark.

"Just hold on to the back of my coat," my chief steward said in his usual slow, mumbling tone. I groped for his coat and seized it, holding on for dear life lest I be devoured by the inky ether that consumed the countryside.

We walked with me holding on as Mr. Oglesby led me up and down dusty hills, across bridges and cattlegates, around unseen obstacles and many corners. While my silent guide led me through the unyielding abyss, my eyes strained for some glimpse of light somewhere. *Oh please, just some lantern glow, some flicker of flame, a candle in the window!* But no, I strained in vain.

Finally, I heard a creak. It seemed that Mr. Oglesby was pushing open a gate in front of us. We proceeded. Suddenly, we were rushed by a herd of "things" that ran around our legs squealing and grunting. My grip tightened. My body tensed. My invisible walking coattail said nothing, and I was afraid to say anything. I then felt a large presence behind me. It made heavy clumping sounds with its feet as it came upon me. My hair stood on end as hot beastly breath poured down my neck under the smothering blanket of starless pitch.

Deliverance came at last when we entered a little shack of a house, and the switch to a weak, low-wattage light bulb was flicked on. Still the harrowing mystery of the night would not be revealed until morning light when Mr. Oglesby and I, adorned in our Sunday best, emerged from his shack to greet a yard full of dusty swine and a nonchalant, wet-nosed mule.

However, there was another mystery of that night that remains with me to this day. How was Mr. Oglesby able to see? The night was so abysmally dark that sight was impossible—at least for me. Somehow, through the years, Mr. Oglesby had developed eyes that could penetrate the sable shroud of a backwoods night in a way that my street-light accustomed eyes could not. What manner of eyes were these? They were special eyes—eyes that were able to see beyond the veil of night.

We need eyes such as these to see God—eyes that are able to see not only through the veil of night, but through the curtain of everyday life. With practice and effort we can develop eyes like these. And we can see God.

• *Chapter 1 Reflection Exercise* •

1. Do you see signs of God's presence in your life? If so, what difference does seeing these signs make for you? If you see no signs, what would you like for God to show you?

2. When is it easiest for you to see God (or at least signs of God's presence)?

3. What is it about God that you "see" more clearly now?

4. What personal steps or changes would help you see God more clearly than you presently do?

5. Take a few moments to consider privately what your life would be like if you had never "seen God" in any way.

And Have You Heard
• *Audition* •

And one called to another and said:
   "Holy, holy, holy is the LORD of hosts;
   the whole earth is full of his glory."
                              (Isaiah 6:3)

Overhearing the Praise

I heard it.

At first it was a low mournful, moaning sound that seeped through the doorway of my bedroom. It would get closer and louder and then suddenly retreat back into a distant corridor. Many times the sound emanated from the kitchen, but it would not remain there. It would float from room to room.

Every now and then the sound would form some barely discernible word or phrase. It had a rhythmic quality and a recurring theme despite its fluctuating, fading volume.

The sound did not concern me. In fact, it was rather comforting. I would, however, wonder about the tears on my mother's face that frequently accompanied the mournful hum.

I later learned that she was only experiencing "a visitation" like she often experienced in church. For my mother was the source of the sound as she moved from room to room tending to the house.

Although I could not name the words masked behind the forlorn sounding notes, I knew she was singing one of those "Old

One Hundreds" that we used to hear at the Visitors' Chapel African Methodist Episcopal Church where I attended as a child or at the Friendship Baptist Church which I joined for three years as a teenager.

She was not singing to me. She was communing with God as she went about her routine chores. But I overheard the conversation between her and the Lord.

Even though I stood outside of her engagement with God, I was yet included in it because I heard her, and the sound I heard during my formative years became an integral part of my spiritual development.

Indeed, because I first overheard my mother's praise and prayer in the rhythms of her song, and because I first overheard the praise and prayers of others like her, I was later able to hear the voice of God.

How, then, can we hear the voice of God in our lives? Again, there are prerequisites. We must begin where Isaiah began, by listening first to the voice of the worshiping community.

As we have already seen, the seraphs in Isaiah's vision formed a worshiping community around the Divine Ruler. Their function as a worshiping community was more significant than their identity as angelic beings.

Isaiah stood outside of this community of worship as a spectator, but on the other hand, at a different level, he was a participant in the worship act because he was there to see and to hear . . . and to respond.

Overhearing worship is a way of sharing in it. It is not adequate sharing, but sharing nevertheless. Furthermore, overhearing worship is a prerequisite to full participation in worship. Full participation in worship opens us to the voice of God.

Worship, of course, can be either a corporate or an individual act. However, the emphasis here is upon the corporate act of worship, worshiping with a community, worshiping in church.

Yes, personal or private worship is a crucial component of our spiritual life and development. Without a private devotional life, corporate worship is impoverished to the point of meaninglessness. Yet without corporate worship, private or personal worship is impoverished to the point of emptiness. Both public and private worship are indispensable requirements for spiritual growth and vitality.

We emphasize corporate worship because the community of faith at worship offers the seeker more opportunities for hearing the voice of God than private worship activity. The opposite may be true for those who are far-travelled in their personal spiritual journeys, but that is a subject awaiting exploration by someone else. Our chief interest is in the beginner pilgrim who asks, "How can I hear the voice of God?"

Isaiah shows us the beginning of the answer.

Listen to the Sound

The cry of the seraphs was not only praise, but it was proclamation; praise by virtue of its content, but proclamation in that the seraphs called to one another—not to God, and especially not to Isaiah. Isaiah heard what they said, but no one was yet speaking directly to him. He was an onlooker, a spectator.

Isaiah stood where we stand before we experience the voice of the Lord. He stood outside the circle of God's called and chosen.

An irony appears here. Isaiah stood outside the circle of God's called and chosen, yet he was a priest of the temple. We know that Isaiah was a priest because when he received his vision he was alone in the temple in the vicinity of the altar. Furthermore, he was well-versed in the language of temple rite and ritual (Isaiah 1:10-14). The exceeding elegance and eloquence of his prose displays a high degree of formal training not available to the commoner. These are the clear signs of a priest. Yet he stood outside the circle of God's consecrated.

Is this not a familiar refrain? Many are in the church. They are active and performing duties. They wear titles, hold offices, and preside over programs and functions. Yet they have not seen the Lord; they have not heard God's voice; they have not felt the spirit and power of worship; they have not sorrowed over nor confessed their sin; they have not experienced forgiveness and the assurance of salvation; they have not heard their call and answered it; and they have not been empowered and sent to serve.

We each must ask, "Am I like Isaiah was? Am I in the church but yet standing outside God's circle of God's called and chosen?" If the answer is "yes," then we can now move on to achieve the necessary changes.

We can begin our pilgrimage toward spiritual transformation where Isaiah began. We can listen to the sound of praise and worship.

Where Our Answer Begins

God is holy. God is exceedingly holy. The holiness of God is that greater aspect of Divine character and being that is separate and removed from, and therefore untouched by, the order of created things. So exceedingly holy is God that the seraphs declared it three times in one breath in their cycle of cries to one another.

We must hear that God is holy and wholeheartedly accept what we have heard. To hear and accept that God is holy is to know who God is. Knowing who God is also means knowing who we are. If God is holy then we are lowly. We are one with the order of created things and are, therefore, apart from the realm of the holy.

We are thrown into crisis. The realization of our separation from the realm of the holy makes us yearn for rapprochement with the Divine. We have a dilemma. We yearn for that which we cannot achieve. This is good. It forces us to be receptive to whatever God does. Without the realization of who we are, we would not be so receptive, and unless we are receptive God will not make the critical move.

Our anxiety increases, however, with the ongoing cry of the seraphs. They identify God as "the Lord of hosts." The word "hosts" (Hebrew: *sabaoth*) refers to the innumerable myriads of angelic beings that inhabit the realm of the Divine.

What? Are they not willing even to share God with the world

of creatures? Is God not also God of both heaven and earth? Yes, God is, but this is beside the point. The point is that there is a wide chasm between us and God, and the key to bridging it is our realization of how wide it is.

The seraphs, nevertheless, offered us something that mitigates against our anxiety with their words "the whole earth is full of his glory." Here they give verbal homage to a truth expressed earlier in the observation, "the hem of his robe filled the temple."

Yes, God is holy. Yes, the Greater Person of God is removed from and untouched by the creaturely realm, yet there is an expression of God's presence that extends throughout the order of created things. Paradoxically, that expression is still holy, but it touches us. It touches us!

Here is where the answer to our dilemma begins. Here is where the assuagement of our anxiety starts. God is everywhere present, a cause of alarm for any who desperately seek to escape God, a cause of assurance for any who diligently seek to find God.

> Where can I go from your spirit?
>   Or where can I flee from your presence?
> If I ascend to heaven, you are there;
>   if I make my bed in Sheol, you are there.
> If I take the wings of the morning
>   and settle at the farthest limits of the sea,
> even there your hand shall lead me,
>   and your right hand shall hold me fast.
>   — Psalm 139:7-10

If God is present everywhere, if God already touches us, then our estrangement from God is not because of any unwillingness on God's part to engage with us. The problem must be with us.

There is something or several things we must do then to allow our encounter with God to complete its course. Let us stay with Isaiah. God showed him what was required; and through him, God will also show us.

To Listen and to Learn

We have learned this much from what we have heard: listening to the voice of the worshiping community is a powerful means of spiritual transformation, especially if we listen to learn two things: who God is and who we are. Neither lesson is possible without the other. We also have seen that the lesson of "who" involves the lesson of "where"; that is, where God is and where we are in relation to God. These are the lessons that make us ready to hear God's voice.

In this way, the voice of the worshiping community becomes the voice of God. The preliminary and proxy sense in which the voice of the worshiping community becomes the voice of God may not be initially satisfying to those of us who search for a deeper discovery of God's voice, but it is still a significant stage in the encounter with God. Besides, the way in which the voice of the worshiping community becomes the voice of God is not meant to be satisfying. It is meant to prepare us for that juncture in our pilgrimage where we hear what God has to say directly to us. Our souls will be satisfied then, and then only.

Call and Response

A church member once shared with me his experience as a youth of casually walking into an African American worship service already in progress. I surmise from his sharing that this was probably during a series of revival services in his community, and that he had decided to look in upon one of the services out of curiosity.

Apparently the service was in full swing when he strolled in. Members of the congregation were caught up in the fervor of praise. Stringed music and the rhythm of percussion instruments rocked the walls of the sanctuary. Hands were raised and waving to escalating shouts of "Hallelujah," "Amen," and "Glory to God," and were clapping to the beat. Feet no longer satisfied to tap the floor rhythmically had already ignited the aisles with dance. Pulpit and pew called out to one another in the antiphonal pattern of praise known as "call and response," a pattern so characteristic of preaching, praise, testimony, and public prayer in African American churches that have not forsaken their heritage. Before long, our then unwary visitor found himself shaking uncontrollably as the same power that swept the room seized him also.

I could say "Amen" to his story. I have had similar experiences. Amazingly, worship and praise such as this which snares even the "innocent" bystander have roots both ancient and divine. Isaiah allowed us one glimpse of this worship legacy when he remembered the call and response praise of the seraphs.

What shall we say then to those who wish to hear the voice of the Lord? We say listen first to the voice of the worshiping community. Furthermore, listen to hear the assembly's declaration of who and where God is, a declaration that also discloses who and where we are. Let us allow ourselves to be drawn into the experience of worship and praise, and in the midst of celebration we shall hear the voice of God.

The worshiping community or church is not the only place to hear God's voice! God's voice is just as unbounded and unrestricted as is God. But we are advising the seeker who longs to hear. Though the worshiping community is not the only place for a divine audition, there is no better place. Come, therefore, to the church and hear what saith the Lord.

A Personal Hearing

I had a personal experience of hearing. It was not at church. It was not in a worship setting at all. It was talent day in Mrs. Kildare's sixth grade class at my elementary School in El Paso, Texas.

I was one among a classroom full of twelve year olds. A few of us sang. A few did skits. A few told jokes and stories. There may have been baton-twirling and other talent acts. Most of us just watched. But one boy in the class, a Latino child named Daniel, decided to do something altogether out of the ordinary even for that day years before the debate over religion in the public school room. He decided to share his Christian testimony. I cannot remember all that he said, but I do remember being awed by his courage and the strength of his conviction as he shared points of his faith with us. I recall the rapt attention of the rest of the class and the reverent respect we gave him as he spoke. I remember the proud support of our teacher as she gave him leave to speak. I remember how much I was changed that day.

I was already part of a worshiping community; and it seemed that from the earliest part of my sojourn as a self-conscious human being I had always been aware of God. But I had never experienced the hearing of faith in a way so poignant and meaningful as that day in my sixth grade class.

I mark that day as a turning point in my Christian journey. I wish that I could find Daniel and thank him for his witness.

Because I heard Daniel, a young representative of a worshiping community, I was later ready to hear the voice of God for myself.

• *Chapter 2 Reflection Exercise* •

1. What answers do you seek or what questions do you have about your spiritual journey at this time in your life?

2. What have you "heard" that has helped or guided you thus far?

3. What is the most meaningful thing you have heard about God?

4. What is the most meaningful thing you have heard about yourself?

5. Can you name times when you have the least difficulty hearing the voice of God?

6. Can you name times when you have the most difficulty hearing the voice of God?

7. What would help you be more open to the voice of God?

All Shook Up
• *Sensation* •

The pivots on the thresholds shook at the voices of those
who called, and the house filled with smoke.

— Isaiah 6:4

I Felt Something

In the mountains of San Bernardino County about five
hundred feet above sea level, I attended another conference on
prayer and healing, one of several events I was involved in that
had to do with spirituality, spiritual gifts, and service. This was
usually a high time of celebration and hope. Music, messages,
ministry, and worship were combined in a way that engendered
healing of the whole self and a sense of empowerment.

Something different occurred for me this time as I sat in one
of that week's several worship celebrations. No one else would
be aware of it. At first, I was not aware of it, but then it dawned
upon me as I sat there listening to the music and witnessing
whatever ministry was going on.

I felt a powerful trembling throughout my being. It was a
strange feeling, as if an electric current of some type were
running through my body. I tried to stop it, but I could not. I
wanted to make sure this was not something that I was causing
to happen.

Whatever it was, it wasn't me. It was some outside power
acting upon me, but not upon me alone. There was a movement

of power throughout the whole sanctuary. Some were singing. Some were praying. Some were weeping. There had been healing, prophecy, and other manifestations of the Spirit's moving.

I was only sensing a Presence. It manifested in me as a shaking. I notice this shaking at other times when there is movement of the Spirit in the midst of a gathering where I am, but it does not occur all the time. It occurs only at certain times, but each time there are other manifestations confirming the fact that what I am feeling is not of my own doing. It is the movement of God.

There may be those skeptical of my experience and even those who refuse to believe what I have described. So be it. I only want to call attention to the dimension of feeling in our spiritual experience. Perhaps some will not feel a shaking or trembling in the midst of worship or devotional exercise. Sensations of warmth, exuberance, ecstasy, and transport have also been recorded as manifestations of spiritual encounter. The skeptic may still dismiss them all.

However, the burden of our question cannot be dismissed. What is that question? It is, "What do you feel in the midst of spiritual life and worship?" Our chief interest is in those who fail to feel anything. Our assumption is that those who fail to feel anything would desire to feel something so that their spiritual life may be enriched. The inquiries then become, "How can I feel the presence of God in my life and worship? What would it mean for me to so feel?" The feeling dimension of Isaiah's experience becomes helpful to us in this matter.

Feeling the Power

Isaiah felt something. We know this only from inference, because Isaiah did not speak directly of personal sensation. He spoke only of the "pivots on the thresholds" shaking from the power of the seraphs' cry while the house filled with smoke.

One of the "thresholds" was the entrance to the Holy of Holies which was behind the altar in the direction that Isaiah was facing. The "pivots" were the five doorposts and crossbeams that supported the olivewood double doors to the Holy of Holies. These doors were overlaid with gold and decorated with gold-plated carvings of cherubim, palm trees, and blossoming flowers (1 Kings 6:31-32).

Another "threshold" or entrance was behind Isaiah. This was the entrance to the nave or Holy Place. The doors of this entrance were cypresswood double doors which were supported by four-sided "pivots" of olivewood. Each door was a folding leaf design overlaid with gold and gold-plated carvings similar to the others (1 Kings 6:33-36).

The doors before and behind Isaiah simply shook at the voice of the angels. Isaiah's observation of this was nothing less than a graphic way of acknowledging that he was shaken too. How could Isaiah be in a room where such power was being generated and not feel the shaking himself?

We therefore have the inference of physical sensation. Isaiah felt the power. Yet Isaiah had more than a physical feeling. He was having, after all, an encounter with God, a spiritual experience. Isaiah surely felt bodily shaken, but he also felt something at levels other than the physical.

Feeling can be no more than a tactile sensation, that is, a message from the nerve endings under our skin to the touch center in the brain: something is hot; something is cold; something is rough, smooth, sharp, hard, soft, and so forth. Feeling can be an emotional mood or response: joy, sorrow, assurance, fear, love, hate, pleasure, anger, and so on. Feeling can be a perception about one's environment: it is safe here; it is dangerous here; it is delightful here; it is depressing here, and so on. Most importantly, feeling can be a sense of spiritual presence and grounding, a feeling of divine support, a feeling of divine companionship, a feeling of divine guidance, and so on. Regardless of how we explain it, feeling is a way of knowing that bypasses the rational processes. We do not stop to think that we are happy; we just know that we are happy. We do not stop to think that we are warm; we just know that we are warm. We do not stop to think that we are afraid; we just know that we are afraid.

Feeling, therefore, gives us access to knowledge that lies beyond the boundaries of reason; beyond the boundaries of what can be seen or heard, analyzed, understood, and explained.

Feeling is knowledge of the heart as opposed to knowledge of the head. So often we are told, however subtly it may be said, that the knowledge of the heart is less reliable and less credible than the knowledge of the head. Examples may be given when those who depended upon intuition or heart-knowledge were proven wrong, sometimes tragically so. Indeed, these examples are valid. However, examples may also be given when those who depended upon reason or head-knowledge were also proven wrong, and, sometimes tragically so.

What must be recognized is that the heart and the head are equal in their ability to produce accurate, reliable, and credible knowledge. They are also equal in their ability to produce error. What is needed to mitigate against error is a balancing of one against the other. There must also be mutual recognition between each of the other's unique suitability for accessing certain aspects of reality. The heart seems to know some things about spiritual reality that the head has difficulty perceiving. The head should, therefore, not dismiss what the heart knows and then purport to substitute a more credible kind of knowledge. Much error results when the head subsumes the role of the heart and the heart takes over the role of the head. No, the head should respect that what the heart knows the heart knows.

The Shout

My own cultural heritage may offer some insight into the role of feeling in spiritual life, particularly in the distinctive way that feeling is expressed in African American worship.

We sometimes speak of "the shout" in African American worship. Despite the usual connotation of the term, this is not merely a vocal outburst. It is a physical expression of joyful or liberating emotion in worship. It may be a vocal reaction. It could also be a dance or some other physical gesture or bodily response.

It is not mere emotionalism. To call it this is a superficial judgment based upon lack of understanding. The shout is a way of "surfacing" the emotions and then "integrating" them with the rational faculty and the body. Shouting in African American worship is a way of becoming a whole person. If this sounds like a goal of psychotherapy, the perception is correct. The shout developed in the crucible of oppression as a way of countering the psychologically debilitating effects of enslavement in the antebellum American South. It was a way of maintaining one's emotional equilibrium in the midst of heart crushing circumstances. The shout, however, adds a spiritual dimension. It brings the heart into communion with the head and the body, and then brings this whole into communion with God. As such, it is not just "letting go" but it is "taking in." It is receiving the healing power of God.

Although the tradition of the shout has been adapted across various cultural lines, it is not expected to occur in all Christian worship settings, nor is it essential that this expression occur in all worship. Its absence does not necessarily indicate a deficiency in a community of faith's spirituality. However, it is essential that some degree of feeling have a role in our encounter with God.

Feeling Is Seeing and Hearing

Although Isaiah's witness sounds like the shaking of his environment and body, it was actually the shaking of his heart. He felt the power of the Divine; it was mediated through the seraphs, but still it was the power of God that Isaiah felt.

What Isaiah felt cannot be separated from what he saw and heard. In fact, the distinctions between seeing, hearing, and feeling in Isaiah's experience are quite artificial. All of the distinctions made here in Isaiah's experience are quite artificial. Although Isaiah's encounter with God can be presented in ten facets and maybe even more, no facet is sufficient in itself to tell the prophet's story.

For Isaiah to see and hear the Lord was also to feel the Lord although he used the image of shaking doorposts to describe it. We can also say that for Isaiah to feel the Lord was also to see and hear the Lord.

The implication, a significant one, is that for us to feel the Lord is also to see and hear the Lord. It is perhaps safe to say that in our spiritual experience, most of our "seeing" and "hearing," if not all of it, is really "feeling." We see, yes, but with the eyes of our hearts. We hear, yes, but with the ears of our hearts.

The heart, of course, is a time-honored metaphor for the human spirit as the seat of "feeling." We must understand, however, that "feeling" in this sense is not mere emotion, but it is a faculty of knowledge. When we speak of seeing and hearing the Lord, we mean that we know the Lord and the Lord's voice at the deepest level of our beings. This level may not be accessible to reason; it is not subject to analysis and neatly packaged explanation, but it is reliable and true. We can depend on it. We can stake our lives on it.

What then does it mean to feel the Lord's presence in our lives, and how can we obtain this experience? To feel the Lord's presence in our lives means only to recognize and acknowledge something that is already here. What else can be done with a feeling of presence other than ignore it or remain unaware of it?

While visiting me in southern California, my son, Michael, age sixteen, experienced his first earthquake late in the night. I also felt it, but it registered only 3.0 on the Richter scale and its epicenter was miles away. Since I had already experienced several stronger earthquakes, I barely took note of it and then quickly forgot it. But the next day, my son excitedly said, "I felt an earthquake last night." The event then resurfaced in my memory.

"Yes, that's right. There was an earthquake last night," I said. It took my son's sharing of his new experience to jog my memory about something that I also felt. How easy it is to feel something and then ignore it. How easy it is also to feel the presence of God and then ignore it.

We are not speaking of trying to produce any particular "manifestations" of God's presence; only to recognize and acknowledge that God is here. God will take care of any manifestations in God's own way and in God's own time.

Recognizing and acknowledging God's presence in our lives is the first step in focusing our spiritual senses. The effect will be tuning out feelings of fragmentation and scattering that contravene our sense of divine accompaniment.

We are speaking of a conscious decision. We need not wait for any flashing lights at noonday nor any thundering voices from above. We are summoned only to decide that from this day on we will consciously recognize and acknowledge the presence of God in our lives. Then we will see and hear God more clearly, then we will feel God more deeply, and the manifestations of God's presence in our lives will be more self-evident.

Is this too much to derive from Isaiah's sensation of shaking doorposts and crossbeams? Only if we can say that Isaiah himself was unshaken. We clearly see, especially in the verses that follow, that Isaiah was all shook up.

The prophet's word is reminiscence of another historical witness to the experience of shaking:

> One night I thought hell would be my portion. I cried unto Him who delighteth to hear the prayers of a poor sinner, and all of a sudden my dungeon shook, my chains flew off, and, glory to God, I cried. My soul was filled. I cried, enough for me—the Savior died.[2]

Richard Allen's "my dungeon shook" further recalls the dungeon shaking moments of Paul and Silas (Acts 16: 25-34), appropriate language for the shaking of his soul, language that is admittedly, a little less cryptic than Isaiah's shaking doorposts.

Critical to our discussion thus far, is the observation that we can know God. We have access to God. We have a faculty uniquely suited to making contact with the Divine. That faculty is feeling-the-knowledge of the heart. We can have all confidence, that whatever knowledge the yearning heart yields about God, that knowledge is trustworthy.

A Gift of Feeling

It was a rare occasion. I perceived that God was summoning me to the work of Christian ministry, but the summons was not

---

[2] Richard Allen, *The Life Experience and Gospel Labors of the Rt. Rev. Richard Allen*, with an introduction by George A. Singleton (Nashville: Abingdon Press, 1960), p. 15.

clear. In any case, the implications of answering the summons were staggering. I was eighteen years old at the time.

On that particular day I wrestled with my call. I wanted God to speak clearly and directly to me so that there would be no doubt in my mind that I was being spoken to by God. How else could I be sure that this is what God really wanted of me?

God did speak to me, but not in an audible voice. God spoke to me in a feeling. A sense of God's presence so powerful and unmistakable came over me that all my fears and concerns evaporated.

It was not through that feeling alone that God spoke to me. There were other confirming signs; but the feeling came first. It was like sensing the presence of someone who had just entered a room. It was not as dramatic as Isaiah's shaking doorposts, but just as meaningful and life-changing.

Rarely, have I experienced this feeling since then. I have certainly never felt God's presence again with that much intensity. Yet the memory of that day when God came so very close remains with me and sustains me through difficult times.

Isaiah showed us in his testimony that feeling is a key component in knowing God. Furthermore, one of the chief resources we have in our sometimes difficult engagement with life is the heartfelt perception of God's powerful presence in our lives.

• *Chapter 3 Reflection Exercise* •

1. Are you primarily a "head" person or a "heart" person?

2. Which do you trust the most, your "head" or your "heart"?

3. Are you satisfied with the level of feeling in your spiritual life? If so, what does your experience of feeling tell you about God? If not, describe the experience of feeling you are seeking.

4. What activities or events do you find most emotionally or spiritually uplifting?

5. What would help you be more open to feeling the presence of God?

Oh No! Exposed!
• *Conviction* •

And I said: "Woe is me! I am lost . . ."
— Isaiah 6:5

Accepting the Truth

I met him in prison. He was an inmate; I was part of a prison ministry team comprised of men who had committed themselves to a three-day weekend with our "brothers on the inside." Our procedure was to enter the prison in the mornings and depart in the evenings.

It was a different kind of fellowship.

We had come to share the meaning of Christian faith to a "captive" audience. Still the participation of these men in our cycle of activities was strictly voluntary. Virtually all of them welcomed the change of routine.

Some, however, had already committed themselves to the Christian faith. One particular inmate was looking forward to being released soon, and he was determined not to repeat the mistakes that had put him in prison.

He acknowledged his wrong. He knew that his sentence to time in prison was justified. He was convicted not only in a court of law, but within himself. He had confronted his error and shortfall, however painful it was, and he had moved on.

He had a female companion who visited him in prison. She

wanted to marry him when he was released. He did not, how-ever, feel worthy of her; and consequently, he was not willing to get married. We established that he loved her. Still he shrunk from the possibility of marriage.

We spoke of his struggle in one of our small group meetings. I offered that perhaps he was failing to trust her love for him and that, furthermore, he had not come to believe that he could be loved without condition. A light came on within him. Again, he experienced conviction, and he accepted the truth.

I was particularly pleased to watch him make progress on his spiritual journey. Clearly, he had reached significant stages of conviction; stages of being confronted by and accepting the truth about himself that also became significant milestones on his journey to spiritual healing and wholeness.

All of us must pass through this stage on our way to trans-formation. Isaiah helps us to realize this.

The Place of Woe

Isaiah could do no more than express an overwhelming sense of shortfall and unworthiness in the light of God's holy presence. His sin-laden inadequacy stood out in jagged relief against the foreground of God's self-disclosure. The shaking of his soul was also the shock of realization over how repugnantly defiled he was in the eyes of the Divine. A sense of abysmally deep despair seized him like the death-grip of a python. His sense of self retreated back into the far recesses of his own dejected soul with no intention of ever emerging again. He was obnoxiously reprobate, and he could not help but know it.

Others have been there, to that place of despair and shame that comes with the realization of who we are and where we stand in our relationship to God.

"Where are you?" This was the question that God called out to disobedient Adam in the genesis of history. Adam responded, "I heard the sound of you in the garden, and I was afraid, because I was naked; and I hid myself" (Genesis 3:9-10).

Not the fear of our nakedness, but the fear of its exposure has plagued our relationship with God from the beginning of the human journey. A tendency to recoil from God's holiness in a fit of self-centered disgust threatens the fulfillment of our spiritual pilgrimage.

Moses' sense of inadequacy and low worth rose up against the call of God and had to be overcome before he finally submitted (Exodus 3:11; 4:10-17).

Guilt and shame overwhelmed David when he was confronted by Nathan the prophet over his adulterous affair with Bathsheba and his conspiracy to take the life of her husband, Uriah (2 Samuel 11:2-27; 12:1-15). The exposure of David's sin drove him to the acknowledgment of a universal plight: "Indeed, I was born guilty, a sinner when my mother conceived me" (Psalm 51:5).

In the New Testament, a Roman centurion sets an extraordinary example of faith when he acknowledges his unworthiness to receive Jesus into his house, requesting instead that Jesus save the life of the centurion's servant with a healing word from afar (Luke 7:1-10).

The African Bishop Augustine of Hippo (354-430 C.E.) was especially plagued by an almost paralyzing sense of unworthiness before the eyes of God:

> Who am I? What kind of man am I?
> What evil have I not done? Or if there is evil that I have not done, what evil is there that I have not spoken? If there is any that I have not spoken, what evil is there that I have not willed to do? But you, O Lord, are good. You are merciful. You saw how deep I was sunk in death, and it was your power that drained dry the well of corruption in the depths of my heart. And all that you asked of me was to deny my own will and accept yours.
> — Saint Augustine, *Confessions* 9.1[3]

Many like Isaiah have been to that place of helpless despair where one cries out, "Woe is me! I am lost!" We must go there also.

---

[3] Saint Augustine, *Confessions*, trans. R. S. Pine-Coffin (New York: Penguin Books, 1961), 181.

Sin and Self-Esteem

Immediately we must respond to a widespread misconception of what is called for in the recognition of our unworthiness before God, that is to say, in the attitude of conviction.

Modern culture, particularly the psychological sciences and self-help disciplines, have taken note of a widespread problem of low self-esteem and self-rejection throughout the population. People are down on themselves and, consequently, down on each other. The results have been an alarming rise in the instances of self-destructive behavior, moral failure, and social irresponsibility.

A new crop of television talk-show hosts has taken the stage and become adept at exploiting incredibly high degrees of self-disdain among guests taken from common walks of life. We are shocked into numbness by the antics of people who have nothing to blame for their misdeeds and mishaps but their own lack of integrity and self-respect.

Our children are showing the signs of low self-evaluation. Substance abuse, sexual promiscuity, sexually-transmitted disease, teen-aged pregnancy, academic failure and truancy, gang activity, drug trafficking, and other pathologies seem rooted in poor self-image. Deficient family and social environments are shown to lie behind most of our children's problems, and this brings us back to the parents who seem no better equipped than their children when it comes to positive selfhood.

Clearly something must be done to help people see their worth and potential. Both young and old must be set free from negative notions of self that are implanted by a vast array of influences and experiences.

Indeed, much has been done on the part of parents, teachers, ministers, doctors, artists, writers, and counselors of various fields and interests to convey a message of worth and esteem to the people, young and old, who need it. Their efforts frequently involve identifying the messages of self-devaluation and their sources. The idea is to expose these messages and their sources so that their influence can be more easily eliminated from our lives. These efforts are usually commendable and effective. They have contributed much to the healing of persons and whole communities.

The problem is that frequently the church or religion is identified as a source of negative messages about human worth. Take, for example, the Christian doctrine of "original sin," the postapostolic belief based upon Romans 5:12-21 that the guilt and sin of Adam has been passed down through the generations to every human being who has been conceived. The idea that we are "born in sin" has been criticized for promoting a sense of unworthiness and self-degradation in people. The religious community, particularly its leadership, is sometimes accused of playing upon people's self-dejection and manipulating them with the promise of forgiveness.

The church is sometimes characterized as a relic of outmoded thinking at the time when people are throwing off the mental shackles of guilt and shame to actualize their full potential.

There is some justification for this harsh judgment of the religious community. The community has sometimes misrepresented the Bible's actual message about the human condition. It is this misrepresentation that is at fault, and not the actual message of the Bible.

The message of the Bible is not that we should feel guilt-ridden and ashamed over who we are, but that we should feel this way over not becoming persons God called us to be.

We can either be our true, authentic selves or be false, unauthentic selves. The former is to be celebrated, the latter is to be lamented.

A shift in a common way of thinking is required here. A common assumption is that our bad self is the way that we are when we are simply being ourselves with no effort being made to be anything else but who we are with no outside influences acting upon us. On the other hand, our good self is the way that God calls us to be.

Actually, it is our good self that responds to God's higher calling. We are authentic personalities, and furthermore, we are harmoniously attuned to God. We walk in accordance with God's will for our lives. We enjoy communion with God, and we know

God. Our relationship with God becomes as basic and natural as that between a child and a loving parent.

The basis of our closeness to God is nowhere better expressed than in the words of the great African bishop:

> You made us for yourself
> and our hearts find no peace
> until they rest in you.
> — Saint Augustine, *Confessions* 1.1[4]

We must hear the Word of God. In effect, that word is that we need not fear those forces that threaten us. We need not be plagued with feelings of anxiety, hopelessness, insecurity, failure, and despair. God offers us the power to be different and to defeat all the negative forces in our lives. God offers us the power to be our true selves, children of God.

However, there is a stage where we must arrive before availing ourselves of this power. We must arrive at the stage where we say, "Woe is me! I am undone!" This stage is necessary, and it can only be achieved when we realize who we really are and where we really stand in relation to God. If we have not yet experienced the transforming power of God's cleansing act, then we can realize only one thing: we are not who God made us to be and wants us to be. We shall see what happened to Isaiah when he reached this stage of despair over being a false self.

An Emerging Trend

We must now revisit certain segments of the psychological sciences and self-help disciplines. For the most part the representatives of these fields communicate a legitimate and effective message from which the religious community can learn.

However, there are bogus representatives of the fields who are content to preach a message of self-acceptance and self-love without first inquiring whether the self they are telling people to

---

[4] Saint Augustine, *Confessions*, trans. R. S. Pine-Coffin (New York: Penguin Books, 1961), 21.

value is a true self. The result has been an emerging trend of tolerating all sorts of strange and self-destructive practices and behaviors in the name of self-love and self-acceptance.

I have even heard pulpit preachers who buy into the trend rise and intone that "Jesus always accepted people just the way they were." This is true, but these preachers somehow always neglect to mention that "Jesus never left people the way that they were."

Today we are seeing the attempt at self-acceptance and self-love without self-surrender to God. We call it an "attempt" because there can be no self-acceptance and self-love without self-surrender to God. What self is there to love and accept without surrender to God? It certainly cannot be the true, authentic self. This attempt can result only in self-delusion and arrogance.

Perhaps our greatest example of someone who found the authentic self to love and accept only through self-surrender is Paul the Apostle:

> So I find it to be a law that when I want to do what is good, evil lies close at hand. For I delight in the law of God in my inmost self, but I see in my members another law at war with the law of my mind, making me captive to the law of sin that dwells in my members. Wretched man that I am! Who will rescue me from this body of death? Thanks be to God through Jesus Christ our Lord!
> — Romans 7:21-25

Paul found the answer to his despair in his own act of self-surrender to Jesus Christ; and about eight centuries earlier, Isaiah found the answer to his despair in surrender to God.

Lesson of the Spider

One day I needed to call a furnace repairman to come to my church parsonage. I had failed repeatedly to get the furnace pilot flame to ignite. He came and had the pilot flame burning in short order. I was curious, of course, about why I could not accomplish this.

He explained the problem. He told me there is a little white spider that is attracted to the smell of gas emanating from the furnace pilot jet. The spider builds its web over the pilot jet and is eventually killed by the gas. The web and dead body of the spider then clog the pilot jet and prevent it from igniting.

I have found this explanation is a helpful analogy for human experience. We sometimes find ourselves attracted to sin in the same way the spider is attracted to the stream of gas. Sin can also be fatal to us, and in many cases it is.

A spider cannot willfully change the behavior that threatens to destroy it, but we can change ours. Change begins with a mood of conviction.

The question is, "Have you been convicted?" If so, then good. It is a necessary stage in your journey. Do not become paralyzed by despair. You are now ready to move on to the next stage. This next stage will bring you even closer to experiencing the transforming power of God in your life.

• *Chapter 4 Reflection Exercise* •

1. What does Paul the Apostle's statement, ". . . all have sinned and fall short of the glory of God" (Romans 3:23) mean to you?

2. How successful do you feel you have been in moving on with your life after experiences of error, shortfall, or sin?

3. Do you feel there are matters weighing upon your heart that need to be surrendered to God? Take a few moments to write these down on paper and then offer them to God in prayer. Without revealing what you wrote you may ask someone to pray with you about these matters as you hold the paper folded in your hand.

4. How should we pray for you as you consider the next step in your spiritual journey?

I Confess! I Confess!
• *Confession* •

"Woe is me! I am lost, for I am a man of unclean lips, and I live among a people of unclean lips; yet my eyes have seen the King, the LORD of hosts!"

— Isaiah 6:5

Putting Out the Trash

I had failed to put out the trash for Monday morning collection two weeks in a row. When I had finally moved the trash cans from the side of the house to the curb, so much trash had accumulated that I had to pile some bags on top of already overfull cans and place some beside the cans.

No one else on the block had as much trash piled in front of their house as I did that day. To make it worse the trash truck did not come first thing that morning, and so the trash sat there for a while for all the neighbors and anyone passing by to see.

I cannot be sure what people thought, but I could imagine my neighbors marvelling at the monument to neglect that I had built on my curb.

And what about the trash truck driver as he approached the pile in his vehicle? After driving down the street making swift work of picking up and dumping one or two partially-filled cans per house, what would he think of the resident who left three weeks' worth of refrigerator's revenge for him to pick up?

Needless to say I was not around to greet him when he came.

What a relief it was when finally the truck came and carried it all away. I felt like a burden had been lifted and I could make a new start. I was no longer ashamed to be seen by my neighbors, and I had a sense of peace about my front yard.

My point in telling this incident is that confessing our sins and shortfall is very much like piling weeks of accumulated trash on the curb. It is embarrassing. It may even be painful and humiliating, but it is necessary to confess our sins and shortfall so that the Divine trash collector may come and take them all away. Peace can then be ours again, and we can make a new start.

I struck upon this analogy when I realized how similar was the way I felt when my trash was hauled away to the way I feel when I confess my sins, wrongs, and mistakes.

And yes, there have been many sins, wrongs, and mistakes: people I have hurt, promises I have broken, lies I have told, trusts I have betrayed, evil things I have thought, anger I have expressed, jealousies I have harbored, injustices I have tolerated, responsibilities I have evaded, laws I have broken, weaknesses I have denied, indiscretions I have covered up, and so on. They have been many, and they have been great sources of personal shame, sorrow, and pain to me.

But when I confess them—first to myself, then to God, and finally to the persons I have wronged—something amazing happens. My sins and shortcomings lose their power to cause me despair. I am able to give them up and become free to live and love again. The practice of confession is a critically important stage in the process of spiritual transformation and renewal.

Piercing the Pretense

Isaiah confessed to being a man of "unclean lips" and living among a people of unclean lips. He both participated in and tolerated the sin of his community.

What Isaiah meant by "unclean lips" (Hebrew: *teme-shepatayim*) has always been an intriguing mystery. It could refer to any one of a variety of sins associated with the mouth:

worshiping false gods; lying, cursing and using obscene language, gossiping, slandering; quarreling, backbiting, bickering, boasting; expressing bigotry; sowing dissension, heresy, and blasphemy; soothsaying, falsely prophesying and witnessing, and perhaps others.

It may even be providential that we do not know specifically what Isaiah meant, so that we would not dismiss from consideration any of the various acts of "unclean lips" that we commit.

On the other hand, we should not take too literally this assignment of sin to the lips. People can hardly have unclean lips without also having unclean minds, unclean hands, unclean feet, unclean ears, and unclean . . .

Isaiah confessed to sin that was thoroughgoing and consuming despite his use of "unclean lips" as an identifying metaphor.

One should not overlook that Isaiah confessed to a corporate sin—the sin of the whole community. This is not to deny the personal and individual dimension of Isaiah's sin; this dimension is present in a very definite and pronounced way in the testimony of Isaiah. However, the corporate aspect of Isaiah's confession is noteworthy because sin of this type is the most easy to deny.

We need look no further than life in contemporary society to illustrate the reality and easy deniability of corporate sin. We all participate in the compromising of moral standards, the escalation of violence in society, the dampening of spirituality, the dishonesty of business and politics, the prevalence of injustice, the promotion of consumerism and materialism, the polluting of the environment, the spread of poverty, the rise in crime, the breakdown of education, the delinquency of children, and the delinquency of parents. We easily deny our personal role in these corporate sins and blame others or "the system."

It was easy also for Isaiah to live in denial about his contribution to the corporate sin of his people until he saw the Lord.

A sure result of an encounter with God is the piercing of all pretense and the exposing of all truth, especially for the one who has the encounter. Denials crumble before the power of the

Divine personality. Responsibility for both personal and corporate sins becomes an inescapable realization; then comes the feeling of being overwhelmed as one wonders what he or she can possibly do in response to all the world's ills. The frustration of powerlessness becomes added to the sorrow of conviction. One actually feels "undone." Confession springs from our heart and mouth like steam through the release valve of a pressure cooker; but then comes a whispered word of peace borne to our hearts by wings of the Spirit: "Despair not; be concerned first with your own transformation. Once you are changed, then your immediate world changes, and these changes in themselves will have far-reaching consequences for the rest of the world."

Grace Is the Answer

Isaiah realized and confessed his complicity in the sins of his people. He knew in that moment who he was and where he stood in relationship to God. He was a false self standing outside the circle of God's chosen and called. Yet Isaiah had seized upon an astonishing paradox, "My eyes have seen the King, the LORD of hosts!"

Clearly, in Isaiah's mind such was never supposed to happen. How could one who has fallen so short and sunk so low be privileged to see the glory of the Lord, and live to tell about it?

There is no logical answer, only a spiritual one. We can only attribute this event to God's grace. Grace is the free, unsolicited, undeserved expression of God's love toward us. Grace brings us to the point where we see God, hear God's voice, and feel God's presence. Grace brings us to the point of confession and takes us beyond.

If you are at the point of confessing your sins in response to your encounter with God, you are a recipient of this marvelous grace.

The Value of Support

Sometimes there is a question about to whom one should confess. The Roman Catholic Church makes regular confession to a priest an expected part of the ongoing life their congregations. There is, generally speaking, no such practice regularly required in Protestant communions. Therefore, Protestants may not be as comfortable with confessing sins to another human being, not even if that person is clergy.

Confessing sins to oneself is often the greatest hurdle. Denial can be an extremely difficult barrier to break through. Intentionally confessing sins to God may not be so difficult after self-ownership of sins is accomplished. But what about to another person?

One observation is needed here. Confession of our sins to self and to God is necessary for freeing ourselves of those sins and experiencing spiritual transformation. We need not share our sins with anyone else to receive the gift of salvation; but we must if we need our brother's or sister's help for our own personal journey. In this case, we must prayerfully search for someone we can trust and who has the skill and ability to help us.

Sharing our problems or shortfall with someone we trust allows them to offer us much needed support in our struggle. Spiritual rebirth or transformation does not mean that all our problems automatically disappear. We still will have struggles and temptations. We still will be subject to mistakes and moments of weakness. A supportive human presence can be valuable.

Yes, God will be with us to support and sustain us, but God also chooses to help us through the presence of other human beings. We must be open to those whom God sends into our lives.

A Liberating Act

Confession is not just "coming clean" about ourselves. Confession is releasing our sins to other hands, the hands of God. It is an act of liberation. It is an act of healing.

Once while being personally prayed for in a service of worship the person praying for me experienced a blockage, that is, something interfering with the healing movement of God's Spirit in my being. He was then led to ask me if I was aware of any unconfessed sin in my life. Admittedly, I had difficulty identifying what it could have been that remained unconfessed, but at least it caused me to think and to examine myself. The more I thought and examined myself the clearer things became, and once they were confessed, the easier it was to experience God's power in my life.

While praying for others myself, I have experienced similar blockages and have been led to ask similar questions. Unconfessed sin blocks the movement of God's Spirit in our lives and hampers our spiritual progress. The singular most important thing we can do to expedite our spiritual change is confess those things in our lives that have caused us to fall short of what God wants. No one said it would be easy.

Once I was invited by a group to submit liturgical material for a Lenten study they were preparing. This occurred in the wake of the Los Angeles civil unrest of 1992. The idea was to publish material that would foster harmony and understanding across racial-cultural lines. I was excited about the project and quickly prepared a piece that I called "An Order of Reconciliation for Historically Estranged Communities." The chief features of the material were litanies of confession on both sides of the historical estrangement. When I reread what I had written, I saw that the material was rather challenging. It called for genuine acts of confession and forgiveness from participants in a service of reconciliation.

I wondered if the piece was too challenging and too hard hitting, and whether I should submit it. Despite my reservations, I sent it in anyway. *Either they were serious about community healing or not*, I thought. If they were, then they would be interested in the litanies. My submission, as of the time of this writing, has not been published. I cannot say why it has not been published. No reason has been given me. There seems to be an uneasy silence about it. In any case, confession is hard. Both being called upon to confess and leading others in confession is hard. We tend to evade the challenge. Spiritual transformation, however, requires confession. Those of us who aspire to be who and what God wants us to be stand therefore with the key to change squarely placed in our hands.

If we say that we have no sin, we deceive ourselves, and the truth is not in us. If we confess our sins, he who is faithful and just will forgive us our sins and cleanse us from all unrighteousness.

— 1 John 1:8-9

True Confession

Isaiah's confession of sin followed immediately upon his vision of the Lord. It was a response to what he had experienced, yet a catalyst for the transformation that was to come. Here we have the difference between false and true confession.

Interestingly, "confession" has become rather trendy in modern times, especially among some public figures who are promoting some cause or concern. Discernment is called for in these cases. It seems that some persons are quick to confess their "sins" for the purpose of showing that they and their cause are credible and trustworthy. They believe that this show of brutal self-evaluation will win people over by changing their skepticism to trust. At times it seems that confession has become a contest among these people vying for our allegiance and support. "The one who confesses the greatest sins wins." This practice sometimes slides into manipulative self-flagellation. The occurrence of this trend among some persuasive personalities within the religious community is particularly regrettable and reprehensible.

Is this confession a sign of genuine response to an encounter with God and a catalyst to personal spiritual transformation? This is the question that must be asked of all acts of confession both public and private. In genuine cases of confession, the answer is not difficult to discern.

When a public confession of sin is given, questions must be asked. Is this an act of contrition for a crime against the public or a betrayal of the public trust? If not, then why make it? If it is only to win support for some cause or concern, then one must question why such a sacred act as confession is being used in this way. Is it to model confessional behavior to those in need of instruction? If so, care must be taken not to give the impression that confession is a badge of honor rather than the humbling of our spirits.

A Personal Confession

One day I stopped praying. As a young Christian I had dedicated myself to the practice of daily prayer and scripture reading. I was fairly consistent through college and the first year or so of seminary.

However, as time went by my dedication to scholarship also increased. I would eventually go on to enroll in a doctoral program and continue more specialized studies beyond graduate school.

But in my pursuit of knowledge, I began to have less time for my devotional life. At least I felt that I had less time for my devotional life. Study and attending classes became more important than prayer. The writings of philosophers and theologians absorbed my interest. My reading of the Bible was displaced by reading books about the Bible.

Soon, I realized something was lost from my life, and it remained lost for a while. My sense of spiritual grounding largely disappeared. My levels of stress and anxiety rose. My vision of God's will for my life became cloudy. My thoughts had not the peaceful clarity of former days. My energy level dropped and depression set in frequently. I felt alone much of the time. I became angry over my failure to achieve certain levels of academic excellence. My spirit felt like a desert. My nerves were frayed. I felt like an exile, and then life fell apart for me. I finally had to forsake the study I so dearly loved.

In the midst of my disappointment and despair, I became convicted of my arrogance in supposing that I had outgrown the need for a daily devotional exercise. I had to confess my sin to myself and to God.

I now realize that a daily time of prayer and scripture reading is just as vital to me as food and water. Confession was for me a difficult stage, but it was a decisive factor in the continuation of my spiritual journey.

• *Chapter 5 Reflection Exercise* •

1. What feelings do talking about confession produce in you?

2. How important has the act of confession been to you on your journey thus far?

3. How important is it to share a confession with another human being?

4. Have you ever trusted anyone enough to share your deepest secrets? If so, tell how this act of sharing made you feel. If not, describe the conditions that must be met for you to trust someone this much.

5. What can the church do to create more opportunities for meaningful confession and the receiving of forgiveness?

Finally Made Clean
• *Cleansing* •

Then one of the seraphs flew to me, holding a live coal
that had been taken from the altar with a pair of tongs.
The seraph touched my mouth with it and said . . .
— Isaiah 6: 6-7

The Reach of Salvation

For a couple of days I had been hearing a constant meowing
coming up through the kitchen floor. Evidently a pregnant cat
had crawled under the house, had her kittens there, and for
some reason abandoned them. I proceeded to the basement and
entered the space under the house through the area where the
hot water heater was hidden. With ducked head and a flashlight
in hand I made my way over to the vent opening where the
feline most likely entered. I could hear the kittens still meowing
back in a cubby hole formed by crossbeams under the house.
They were so far back in the hole I could not reach them. I had
not the slightest idea of how to resolve the problem. If I did not
get the kittens out, they would die under my house and the end
of this story would be worse than the beginning. Realizing that
the situation was beyond my ability, I called animal control who
informed me that they would be glad to come get the kittens,
but I would have to be the one to get them out from under
my house. Returning to the dark cavern under my house did

not reveal any solutions to me. It was a frustrating set of circumstances. Eventually the meowing ceased. The worst had happened. For the next week or so, my nose and I would have to live with what followed.

Since then I have told this story more than once in church, and I have always followed it with this question and statement, "What if God could not reach us in a time of crisis the way that I could not reach those kittens? The consequences would be disastrous."

Isaiah stood abandoned by his own self-deception and alone in the pit of corruption, his guilt overwhelming him like a flood, and his spirit being asphyxiated in the deadly grip of despair. He needed the healing, cleansing touch of God to restore his soul and revive his spirit. Could God reach him after he had sunk so low in the quagmire of sin?

As those who have stood or still stand where Isaiah stood, we have more than a passing interest in the answer. We therefore search for assurance in the testimony of Isaiah.

Fire of Purging

As the divine manifestation to Isaiah continued to unfold, there was a dramatic shift in the role of the seraphs. They first were attendant upon God and raised their voices to worship God with praise. Now, in response to Isaiah's confession of sin, one of them, through some means of communication that was inaccessible to Isaiah, was dispatched to the altar to retrieve with tongs a burning coal with which to touch Isaiah's lips.

From praising God to purifying Isaiah; this was an extraordinary shift in the role of the seraphs.

This experience speaks to the exalted character of God in the vision of Isaiah. A wide chasm remains between the holiness of God and the creaturely nature of human beings. God, in the integrity of the Divine being, remains high and removed from contact with the creaturely realm. An intermediary is therefore required to bridge the wide gap between God and human. This intermediary function is performed by a seraph.

This experience also speaks to the nature of the seraphs.

They are divine beings, yet close enough to humans to bridge the gap between humans and God. Indeed, they appear in some respects to be closer to humans than they are to God, since even they must wrap themselves in a shroud of wings in the presence of God. Yet it is important to recognize their role as extensions or embodiments of God. The seraphs were also the presence of God; and, as such, they were symbolically parallel to the hem of God's robe which filled the temple.

The approach of the seraph was therefore the approach of God. The cleansing touch of the seraph was the cleansing touch of God. Yet it was not a direct touch. It was with a burning coal taken from the altar with a pair of tongs. The cleansing power of fire became the core symbol in the purging of Isaiah's sin. Isaiah's guilt and sin were not just washed away, they were burned away, implying a thoroughgoing experience of cleansing.

Fire! Heat! Power! We feel the intensity of the scene, and the intensity is underscored by the presence of tongs in the hand of the seraph. The suggestion is that without the tongs the fiery coal would have seared the seraph, traumatizing the angel's being in some mysterious way so that the coal could not be conveyed to Isaiah's lips.

Here we have another paradox: a coal too hot for the angel to handle, yet it does not hurt or burn the lips of the human. What does it show? It shows that even though this is a coal taken from the altar of the Holy Place, it burned not with ordinary fire, but with a supernatural fire.

We can now see that the presence of the tongs was not really indicative of a threat to the being of the seraph but to disclose contact between two qualitatively different realms, the realms of the supernatural and the natural. The seraph and the fire, and perhaps even the coal itself were from the same realm; and so the coal was handled as it would be if a human were handling a burning hot coal from the natural realm—very carefully and with tongs. Isaiah was therefore exposed to a supernatural fire, a spiritual fire, and the result was the sanctification of his soul.

The fire of the coal, and perhaps even the coal itself was another symbol for the presence of God. It was not merely a burning coal that touched the lips of Isaiah, it was the presence of God that touched the lips of Isaiah.

Distinctions between God, robe, seraphs, and fiery coal eventually disappear in our engagement with Isaiah's vision. It is God all the way who engages the prophet; but the distinctions must quickly reappear because the mystery of God's being and Isaiah's experience is too unfathomable to explain without them.

All of this is to say that it is God who meets us at the bottom of our well and raises us to new spiritual heights. It is God who embraces us with our grit and grime and breaks forth with cleansing power.

Meaning of Salvation

But what is it that we experience when we are cleansed by God? There have been other ways of asking this question: What does it mean to be saved? to be justified? to be sanctified? to be born again? to be regenerated? to be converted? to be redeemed? to be delivered? to have a spiritual or religious experience? The ways of asking the question are as varied as the cultures and histories of the communities that are asking, and so are ways of answering.

Common aspects can be gleaned, however, from the variety of answers. For the sake of focus we shall speak of terms of salvation or being saved. We shall furthermore orient our answer to the experience of Isaiah.

Salvation means the erasing of our guilt and sin. It is as though they never happened. We, of course, may have difficulty forgetting the sordidness of our past. Putting our past behind us and moving on is a challenge we have to meet. It is not, however, a challenge for God, who, after all, is the one who judges us. For God, the guilt and sin of our former days become nonexistent in the act of salvation. When we are saved, we are new people and we make a new start.

Salvation means a radical reorientation of our core personality. A shift in desire occurs from former passions and obsessions to new aspirations and aims. Principles and values which were at best pedestrian are replaced by higher standards of behavior and life. An outlook on living that was bland at best is discarded for a piercing vision of the beauty of life. Delusions of self-sufficiency are vanquished by the newly perceived reality of a Mighty Hand that guides our destiny. Fears and dreads that haunted our hearts are now driven out by a flood of assurance. The hollowness within has been exchanged for a vitalizing gift of power. We are not the same.

We would have to jump ahead to hear how the seraph confirmed the preceding for Isaiah; and so for now we simply observe that the event of salvation had indeed already happened for Isaiah immediately with the application of the fiery cleansing coal.

Invitation Accepted

There is an ancient question that continues to burn in the hearts of men and women, "What must I do to be saved?" (cf. Acts 16:30). When the jailer of Philippi asked this question, Paul and Silas responded, "Believe on the Lord Jesus, and you will be saved, you and your household" (Acts 16:31). We commend this selfsame answer to any and all who ask the question.

However, we can still learn from Isaiah what this answer means even though God's revelation to Isaiah predated God's revelation in Jesus Christ by eight centuries. The response required of Isaiah was essentially the same as that required for the Philippian jailer. Each had to humbly accept God's gift of cleansing.

We have already spoken of the need to develop spiritual eyes, to listen first for the voice of God in the voice of the worshiping community, to be open to feeling, to realize who we are and where we stand in relationship to God, but now we speak of accepting the divine gift of cleansing.

The former acts were simply ways of inviting God's entry into our lives. This act of accepting is to allow God to do what we have invited God to do. None of this is a formula that automatically results in salvation. Formulas or "steps" to being saved are helpful guidelines, and we should not be overly critical of them; however, we must be careful not to reduce salvation to a matter of mechanics only. There must be a certain disposition or readiness of heart regardless of what "steps" are followed. God responds to this readiness of heart, not because God has to, but because God desires to. God, in fact, responds to this readiness of heart with saving grace even if all the steps have not been followed.

Isaiah's unique experience is most enlightening for it shows that God responds to the opportunity to save us even if that opportunity exists without our first extending to God an invitation. Observe that Isaiah did not consciously extend God an invitation to come in the way that God came on that day. But God came because the opportunity was there. Isaiah was somehow ready. How much more so will God come to save us if we invite God to do so. However, after God accepts our invitation, we must accept God's response to our invitation.

Accepting God's response is a matter of the heart's being ready to accept. We must lay aside all reservations. We must stop beating ourselves up over past mistakes. We must discard feelings of guilt and unworthiness. We must stop worrying about how our lives will be changed. We must forget about how our family and friends would react. And we certainly need to stop worrying about whether we can complete the journey once we begin our new lives. Only one thing is required now—simply accept the gift of cleansing that God offers. God will take care of the rest.

Self and Salvation

We must explore another question about the nature of salvation. Is salvation the same as being "self-actualized"? The psychological sciences and self-help disciplines use the term "self-actualized" or some similar term to denote that stage in life when one has found meaning and purpose, stability and direction, confidence and self-acceptance in life. Counseling and helping professionals design their practices and programs to assist people in achieving this level of development in their lives. This is laudable and good. It is to be applauded, encouraged, and supported. Much of what the counseling and helping professions do is compatible with the ministry and message of spiritual transformation.

However, there is a difference. We speak not of being self-actualized, but "God-actualized." There is much that we can achieve through the adjusting of our attitudes and the changing of our thinking and behavior, but in the end there is a stage in life that cannot be achieved by our efforts. It can be bestowed upon us only by an outside power, and that power is God. This stage involves the transformation of the human personality at the very core of our being. Such a thoroughgoing transformation can be brought about only by the cleansing power of God.

Salvation also involves a dimension that transcends the purview of the psychological sciences and self-help disciplines. It is a dimension that is unique to spiritual study and practice, and must not be shoved aside in the name of rational discourse. This is the dimension of eternal life. Salvation ultimately means that we will live forever in the world beyond this one. We are not speaking merely of "living on the memory of God" or "becoming one with the great cosmic ocean." These are only a couple of the alternative concepts for the way eternal life is understood in this discussion. We are speaking of the subjective, self-conscious survival of our personhood and personality in individual bodily form of some type after the cessation of all physical functions.

Belief in God means belief in life beyond death. God is the one who promises life beyond death. The reality of life beyond death and our belief in it is indeed rooted in the character of God.

God and Salvation

Biblical faith perceives and proclaims that God is a self-aware being possessing a unique integrity and individuality who interacts with an environment, pursues interests, and seeks relationships with others. God is not a bodily or physical self in the way that human beings are, but a self nevertheless.

God is the Supreme Self. This means that God is sur-passingly excellent in being, character, and power. In short, the essence of God is supreme love and power. Supreme love mandates that life continues for those locked in embrace with the Everlasting God. Supreme power wills to make it so. The God who loves so much that our lives are created here in the first place, is also able to recreate our lives in the world to come. The question is not whether God can give us life. God has already shown that. Rather the question is whether God will give us life. Our life with God lived so far already answers this question with a resounding "Yes."

We have just spoken of salvation in its ultimate and final sense, but salvation is also a present reality in the here and now for those of us who have accepted it. We have been cleansed and renewed. We own our salvation now in the midst of our ongoing struggles and pains; but the intensity of our struggle and pain is ameliorated by the anticipation of final victory over the forces of death and evil.

With the cleansing of Isaiah we have reached the watershed of his spiritual experience. We have been shown the watershed of our own spiritual pilgrimage should we choose to arrive there. When we accept cleansing, the gift of new life will be ours.

Imprint of the Creator

While on assignment as Bible Teacher for the School of Christian Mission in Hawaii, I had opportunity to take in some of the indescribable beauty of those gleaming islands. I also had a chance to learn about unique natural resources that are indigenous to that place.

One such resource was the candlenut (kukui) tree which grew outside of the place where I stayed. I was fascinated by the explanation I heard concerning the way ancient and contemporary Hawaiians used the properties of this tree. It yields a bulbous type of fruit that produces a blazing torch light when ignited. Its sap, however, can be refined into a salt-like preservative for food or may be used as a medicine for various ailments.

This one tree can be used to produce light, to heal, and to save. What a testament that was to its creator! Here was nature itself in the midst of an island paradise bearing the very imprint of the character of God who also grants us light, healing, and salvation for our souls. I could not help but be struck by the prodigy before me, particularly at that time when I was teaching the Gospel of John, where the language of light, healing, and salvation figure so prominently.

Isaiah encountered the God of light, healing, and salvation. As we follow the steps of his pilgrimage, this stage of our journey may prove to be the most wonderful of all.

• *Chapter 6 Reflection Exercise* •

1. Are there any human models of spiritual life in your past you especially admire? If so, what qualities about them do you admire the most?

2. If your answer to the first question was "no," then what qualities would you find admirable anyway?

3. Can you recall anyone in your past whose spiritual walk has influenced your life? If so, in what ways have that person influenced you?

4. If you answered "no" to the previous question, who or what has influenced your life?

5. In what ways have you changed on your spiritual journey?

6. Does the term "salvation" have any significance in your life?

You're All Right, Now
• *Confirmation* •

"Now that this has touched your lips, your guilt has departed and your sin is blotted out."
— Isaiah 6:7

God's Whisper

I found interesting parallels between the conversation I was having and one I had six months earlier. I was speaking to a woman who sought counsel as she struggled with her divine call to more intentional service in and through the church of Jesus Christ. She was not being called to ordained ministry, but she was being called nevertheless to a more committed deployment of her gifts in the service of the Lord.

Her problem was fear of how responding to her call would affect her family life, particularly the relationship between herself and her husband. This fear was an insight that was not apparent to me at first and it was not something she openly declared. However, it was "whispered" to me as we conversed, and when I expressed her fear, it became for her a confirming word.

Deep within she knew this to be the case, but apparently needed someone else to say it. With her fear exposed on the surface of her consciousness, she then felt empowered to confront it and resolve her conflict of feelings. She was ready to make a full commitment to her call a few days later.

Six months earlier I was in conversation with another woman who was also struggling with her divine call; however, her call was to the ordained ministry. Her call was unmistakable and undeniable, nevertheless she was hesitant to answer for fear of how responding to her call would disrupt the present course of her life. Again, I did not know her fear at first and she did not immediately reveal it. Insight into her struggle came as a "whisper" in the course of listening. When I shared what I received, it became for her a confirming word. Once she was told what she already knew deep within, she was able to make her life-changing decision.

Two women, one called by God to dedicated lay service, the other called by God to ordained ministry, and there I was on both occasions burdened with the task of being an instrument of confirmation for these daughters of Zion. What could I possibly know about God's will for these women?

Others have confirmed God's word to me in the past. I have always been thankful for the help that I received from others in recognizing the voice of God in my life; but to find myself summoned to this confirming role was frightening. What if I found myself with nothing to offer but a blank expression? For a while, as I listened, a blank expression was all that I could offer. Thank God for the "whisper," a small miracle of insight, undoubtedly a gift from the Spirit, that enabled me to fulfill my role. God used my voice to confirm what they already felt or experienced below the level of conscious reflection. By so doing God also confirmed my call to this particular role.

God's call to service or ministry is not the only divine act that God confirms. We shall see that God confirms a variety of acts in God's dealings with human beings. In Isaiah's case, confirmation meant the assurance that God's work of salvation had been accomplished in the prophet's life. We can also use the term confirmation more broadly to mean God's act of assuring us that God is with us on our life's journey and in the challenges we face.

God's Confirming Acts

Confirmation has always been a component in God's dealing with human beings. God confirmed the divine promise to bless Abraham with countless descendants after Abraham demonstrated radical obedience to the will of God (Genesis 22:1-18).

God confirmed the divine presence and will for Moses and the people of Israel through numerous signs and wonders. Among them were the ten plagues visited upon Egypt for Pharaoh's refusal to set the Israelites free (Exodus 7:8-11:10).

God confirmed the promise of victory to the army of Gideon before they went out to defeat the Midianites with outnumbered forces (Judges 6:36-40).

God confirmed the cleansing of Isaiah through the pronouncement of the seraph (Isaiah 6:7).

And then, jumping ahead to the New Testament, the Resurrection of Jesus is confirmed by the appearance of angels at the tomb (Matthew 28:1-8; Mark 16:5-7; Luke 24:1-4) and by Jesus' own appearance in the gathering place of the disciples (Matthew 28:16-18; Mark 16:14; Luke 24:36-43; John 20:19-29).

Not to be overlooked is the confirming appearance of the resurrected Jesus to Mary Magdalene who, almost eight centuries after Isaiah, also said, "I have seen the Lord" (John 20:18 ; cf. Matthew 28:9; Mark 16:9).

Many other cases of God's confirming acts can be gleaned from the Holy Scriptures.

In Isaiah's case, God confirmed the removal of guilt and sin from the prophet's very being. It was a deed already accomplished, but God wanted Isaiah to know that it was done. In this way, confirmation became a gift to Isaiah. It became a wellspring of inner peace, joy, and confidence; and these spiritual resources in turn became the core elements in Isaiah's heart around which prophetic energy would be marshalled for the task ahead.

The experience of confirmation means inner strength. Once it is established in our heart of hearts that we are newly formed in God, we are greatly reinforced against the hostilities of life. Negative circumstances and situations may press upon us and hem us in, but they cannot extend their reach to our hearts. Our hearts are shielded by the force field of assurance. We are God's and God is ours.

Isaiah's experience of confirmation was demonstration of a truth that reveals itself over and over in the biblical record. God summons us to faith, but never to "blind faith." The faith that God calls us to is a faith grounded in God's confirming acts.

Yes, it is wrong to expect God to prove the presence and power of the Divine Self first and then we believe. This would be a deficient faith at best. First we believe, then God confirms our faith, and our faith is further reinforced by what God has done.

In the gospel, the disciple Thomas refuses to believe that the Lord Jesus is risen until he is able to inspect the nail wounds in Jesus' hands and the spear wound in his side. Jesus appears and allows Thomas to do just that, after which Thomas believes (John 20:24-28). However, it appears that Thomas has missed out on something valuable; and this is implied in the words of Jesus:

> Have you believed because you have seen me? Blessed are those who have not seen and yet have come to believe.
>
> — John 20:29

Why are those who have believed without seeing more blessed than those who have believed by seeing? This would seem to go against common sense. Surely, those who have eyewitness evidence are on more solid ground than those who do not; and since they do is this not a more blessed state? Apparently not in the eyes of Jesus.

Those who believe only by seeing are dependent upon their physical eyes for the creation of faith, and their faith is therefore as limited as their human sight. Those who believe without seeing have learned to depend upon a different set of eyes, namely, their "spiritual eyes"; and "spiritual eyes" can see abundantly more than physical eyes. Furthermore, while the seeing power of the physical eyes diminishes with time, the power of the spiritual eyes continues to increase. Faith based upon spiritual sight, therefore, has unlimited potential for development. This potential for unlimited development is further enhanced and expedited by God's act of confirmation.

The addition of confirmation to faith is far more enriching than the addition of confirmation to no-faith. The former results in the expansion of spiritual vision, and this in turn means the expansion of personal spiritual power in life and living. The latter may result in faith, but it is the kind of faith that can never achieve the depth and power of the former.

Thomas received confirmation that the Lord was risen, but it was not his faith that was confirmed; only what he heard. Surely, his experience resulted in faith, but it was the kind of faith that would always limp along, dependent upon physical evidence. Perhaps, this is one reason why we hear no more of Thomas and some of the others after the Gospel of John.[5]

We are summoned, therefore, to a confirmed faith, a faith reinforced and enriched by God's self-disclosure and demonstration of power. This is nowhere better underscored than in the story of Isaiah.

God Speaks First

Isaiah's experience of confirmation was also demonstration of the truth that God never leaves us without assurance of what God has done. This is especially germane in the case of personal salvation. As a young Christian I was frequently troubled by uncertainty over whether or not I was saved, and earnestly desired and prayed for some sign of confirmation. In time,

---

[5] There is, however, a Coptic version of The Gospel of Thomas, dated 400 C.E. and based upon a Greek original dated 150 C.E., that was discovered among the Nag Hammadi texts of Upper Egypt in 1945–6. There are also The Acts of Thomas, a Syriac text composed in Edessa during the first half of the third century, The Apocalypse of Thomas, a Latin text originating at the end of the fourth century, and The Infancy Gospel of Thomas, a work of late date that has been translated into several ancient languages. These are apocryphal works written by unknown authors long after the deaths of the original apostles.

however, I learned to recognize confirming signs that were already there. Indeed, I came to realize that both worry over personal salvation and the desire for confirmation were in themselves confirming signs of my personal salvation.

Isaiah's experience of confirmation is illustration of yet one other verity. When God confirms either an accomplished deed in our lives or a message to us, God will speak directly to us. I do not wish to neglect this important point in this day of religious hucksterism and deception. God will not send anyone to tell us something that God has not already told us unless it is to educate us in some way. God will not send anyone to require of us any commitment of our selves, our time, our money, or any other of our resources unless God first tells us. Anyone who claims to "speak for God" about something that God has not already told us is deservedly suspect. When God speaks to us first, then anyone who comes afterward to say the same thing adds only further confirmation. God does indeed send people in our lives to do this very thing. But God will not leave us vulnerable to false prophets and deceivers. God will in some way speak to us first so that we can confirm the truth of whatever else we hear.

God may speak to us through a feeling deep within our hearts. God may also speak to us through a text of scripture, the words of a hymn, an overheard prayer, the example of a friend, a dream in the night, the outcome of a current event, a flash of insight, trusted advice, personal experience, and so on. In whatever way God chooses, God speaks, and we must learn to listen.

It is important to see that, for Isaiah, more was confirmed on that day than his personal cleansing and salvation. Yes, it was ostensibly the removal of his guilt and sin that was confirmed by the angel, but the very shape and direction of his life from then on was also confirmed.

We have already spoken about listening for the voice of God. This has been an extension of that discussion. Let us listen, and what God designs for us in our lives will be made clear.

A Confirming Message

We were gathered in front of the Germiston Central Methodist Church of Germiston, South Africa. We had completed our task of leading the first Emmaus weekend in South Africa and were now preparing to catch our bus back to Jan Smuts Airport where we would catch a KLM flight back to the United States.[6]

My spirit was heavy. Even though the day we were leaving was the very day that South Africa had repealed the Separate Amenities Act of 1953 ending the segregation of public facilities in South Africa, I was still depressed by what I had been seeing for the past twenty-one days of the effects of South Africa's apartheid system. In retrospect, I had allowed myself to become too emotional in my response to what I heard and saw in South Africa. I should have been more objective and levelheaded.

While standing there in front of Germiston Church I was approached by an elderly resident of South Africa. His tattered clothes and rough appearance indicated that he was a tragic product of South Africa's racist legacy. Like many of the broken drifters I encounter at home in Los Angeles, he was looking for spare change.

However, a peculiar twist occurred in this developing episode, when after greeting me, the man launched into a monologue. As he spoke, my ears strained to penetrate his thick accent and make sense of his broken English. His mastery of English was, of course, far superior to my Xhosa or Zulu, especially since my knowledge of these languages was nonexistent. Nevertheless, understanding him was a difficult challenge. Whatever he was saying, he was inspired. His voice and gestures were full of animation and enthusiasm as he obviously related to me a story of some type. Meanwhile, I continued to strain to pick out bits and pieces of what he was saying in an attempt to discern some recognizable story line.

---

[6] "The Walk to Emmaus" is a 72-hour spiritual renewal weekend sponsored by the Upper Room and designed to equip Christians for more effective service in their local churches and communities.

And then a breakthrough occurred. I am not sure what triggered the breakthrough, but suddenly I recognized the story he was telling me. It was probably because I was standing in front of the church, and he thought I was of the church that he had chosen to tell me a story straight out of the Old Testament, the story of Joshua and the Battle of Jericho (Joshua 6:1-21)!

Josh-ua fit de bat-tle of Jer-i-cho, Jer-i-cho, Jer-i-cho;
Josh-ua fit de bat-tle of Jer-i-cho, an' de walls come
tumb-lin' down. down.
— African American spiritual[7]

It was not until he was nearing the end of the story that I realized what he had been saying to me, but what a joy it was to both of us when the light of understanding came on.

When he had finished I gave him the last rand I had in my pocket. I had planned to save my South African currency as a souvenir, but I felt he had greater need for it.

Soon we were on the bus and then on the plane. I believe I was somewhere between Nairobi and Amsterdam, still heavy in spirit, when I remembered the encounter with my storyteller from the streets of South Africa. Suddenly again, a light came on in my head.

"Wait a minute! That was no ordinary encounter. That man was a messenger, and through him God was trying to tell me something."

"Do not despair. I've got South Africa surrounded, and the walls are about to come tumbling down!"

Yes. Yes. I knew that already. Deep within I knew that. But now it was confirmed. And several years later, it was confirmed again, with the ascendancy of Nelson Mandela to the Presidency of South Africa.

Yes, God had South Africa surrounded. And God had the Soviet Union surrounded! And God had the Berlin Wall

---

[7] "Joshua Fit de Battle of Jericho," *Songs of Zion* (Nashville: Abingdon Press, 1981): 96.

surrounded! And God had the United States surrounded! And God had Los Angeles surrounded! And God still has all of us surrounded! And soon the walls will come tumbling down!

There were about six centuries between Joshua and Isaiah, but in a way the walls came tumbling down for Isaiah as well, and it was confirmed through the voice of the angel. If we listen, God will confirm what God is doing in our lives also, and then, we can walk with greater assurance.

• *Chapter 7 Reflection Exercise* •

1.   Did reading this chapter on confirmation confirm anything that you have been feeling in your heart? If so, what?

2.   Often in retrospect we recognize God's confirmation in our lives. That is, when we look back, we see God leading us, encouraging us, and affirming us. Are there any other confirming experiences that you have had on your journey? Please share at least one of them.

3.   Is there anything about your spiritual life or pilgrimage for which you still seek confirmation? Please share it if you are comfortable doing so.

4.   Are you able at this present moment to confirm something that someone in this room has questioned? If so, please share the insight with the group.

Who Will Go?
• *Calling* •

Then I heard the voice of the LORD saying, "Whom shall I send, and who will go for us?"

— Isaiah 6:8

Uniquely Suited

I did not know there was a shoplifter among us. I had been standing patiently in line at the supermarket blissfully unaware of any suspicious activity. I paid for my grocery item and proceeded to exit the store behind a few other people.

Suddenly, barreling down one of the aisles comes three hundred pounds of unbridled corpulent fury discharged like a cannonball from the shadowy quarters of the security surveillance room.

The human behemoth swoops down upon a man off to my side, and in swift, fluid motion grabs him by the belt at the small of his back, lifts him off the floor, and with his prey in tow vanishes beyond the pickled okra, back into the secret recesses of the supermarket behind the steel doors marked "Employees Only."

I thought to myself after the shock of the scene wore off, *Now there was a man uniquely suited for his calling. What security force would not delight to have such a huge embodiment of dedicated loss control on its staff?*

Members of my congregation thought this story amusing when I shared it with them, but there are some serious aspects to be acknowledged here. First, our shoplifter was in serious trouble and the consequences of his actions could only be regrettable. Second, the point about being uniquely suited for a calling is indeed a serious one that deserves all consideration.

All of us have a calling, that is to say, a vocation to which God has summoned us; and furthermore, God has uniquely equipped each of us for the peculiar calling that is ours. Admittedly, calling, as it is understood here, means something more specific than the sense in which it was applied to the security guard in our illustration above.

Our calling is the personal way that we actively fulfill God's plan for and work among the human family. It is by definition an expression of our spirituality and occurs in the context of the living out of our faith. Ways of fulfilling our calling are as varied as the individuals who are called.

There are certainly more ways to fulfill God's calling than through ordained ministry. Indeed, ordained ministers are not the only ones who are called by God to service. Paul the Apostle acknowledged a variety of gifts, services, and activities to which we are called (1 Corinthians 12:4-6), and even concluded his case with the question,

> Are all apostles? Are all prophets? Are all teachers? Do all work miracles? Do all possess gifts of healing? Do all speak in tongues? Do all interpret?
> — 1 Corinthians 12:29-30

Clearly, if there are a variety of works and ministries that God calls us to, then it is incumbent upon each one of us to seek out our calling and pursue it with diligence.

The Voice of God

Isaiah heard God's call, but it was in the form of a question. Observe the significance of this question form of the call: God's call is not a command but an invitation, requiring a freewill decision to accept and respond. God simply will not force a vocation upon us, but rather, offers it to us as an avenue to the joy and fulfillment of purposeful living. Our calling is placed before us without threat or coercion. If we refuse it, we cheat ourselves out of a depth of enrichment in life that can only come from obedience. God places the wealth of the world at the hands of the obedient and bestows the gift of eternity on top of that. Our chance for this wealth is tied up with our decision whether or not to accept God's offer of vocation.

Notable is the fact that it was God who spoke this time in Isaiah's hearing and not one of the seraphs; and it would be God who spoke from then on. The point is that our calling to ministry or service comes directly from God and from no one else.

I speak of my own calling with some hesitancy because I want to avoid the impression that the calling to ordained ministry is the only divine calling there is. It is not. There are numerous lay ministries and services that are just as divine in origin and nature as any field of ordained ministry. Nevertheless, prior to the receiving of my calling, I heard from many people, including several clergy, who told me that I was to preach. They could see the signs. Indeed, God was speaking through them to me. Still, their voices were not the direct voice of God. I needed to hear from God and not just an intermediary.

Although Isaiah's call was heard directly from God, it was not spoken directly to Isaiah. Here is yet another one of the paradoxes that has confronted us throughout this narrative. God was overheard speaking to the heavenly court, asking in part, "Who will go for us?" We have seen this divine "us" before in the creation of humanity:

> Then God said, "Let us make humankind in our image, according to our likeness."
>
> — Genesis 1:26

Elsewhere we have observed that this use of "us" discloses God's nature as a social being,[8] but in this case, the first person plural is the divine audience of God; for God is too high and far removed from the realm of creaturely existence to have a human audience. Yet, paradoxically, the words of God were intended for a human audience, namely, Isaiah.

These paradoxes are meant only to hold God's holiness and God's nearness to us in tension. We cannot smooth them out nor should we try. Still it is God's voice that we hear in the moment of calling, and it is only God's voice that we should seek. Modern expressions of spirituality that purport to hear the voices of "angels," "ancients," or "spirit-guides" pose a particular danger to those seduced by them. To seek any voice other than that of God is to expose ourselves to the voice of deception, which in turn places our spiritual development in jeopardy.

Divinely Equipped

Isaiah's calling followed immediately upon receiving confirmation of his cleansing. Cleansing itself was part of Isaiah's equipping process. As we have seen, cleansing was not simply the removal of guilt and sin, but the creation of inner resources that Isaiah would need for the prophetic task.

God equips us for our calling. This equipment is constituted not only by inner resources of the spirit, but also by natural abilities, aptitudes, and talents. God empowers our whole selves for the vocations to which we are called.

One day while visiting the dentist I learned that I had an extra tooth in my mouth. Most adults have only thirty-two teeth, but I had thirty-three at the time. My dentist explained that I still had one of my childhood teeth in place. Usually, when the adult teeth grow in they crowd out all the childhood teeth for lack of room in the mouth. So I asked why this did not happen for me. My dentist said, "You have an extra big mouth."

---

[8] See Kenneth L. Waters Sr. *Afrocentric Sermons: The Beauty of Blackness in the Bible* with a foreword by Cain Hope Felder (Valley Forge: Judson Press, 1993), pp.23–24. Here I speak to this point in my sermon "Made in God's Image."

Ah ha! The sure sign of anyone called and equipped for preaching. A good test may be to inspect all the preachers among us and see how many of them have extra big mouths.

All joking aside, however, our natural gifts and graces are among the attributes indicating our suitability for a particular calling.

How then do we know what our calling is? We can discern our callings by answering several questions:

1. What do I hear God saying to me?
2. What form of activity or expression comes easily for me?
3. What is it that I love to do?
4. What are my natural gifts, graces, and talents?
5. What does my family or community affirm about me?
6. What already existing areas of service seem suitable for me?
7. What areas of service can I create if there appear to be none already suitable for me?
8. What do I hear God saying to me?

The order in which we deal with these questions is not very important; however, it is important that we begin and end with the question of what we hear God saying to us.

Do Something

It may be helpful also to share something I have heard said in church, "God calls those who are already doing something." A review of the biblical record seems to bear this out. God called Moses while he was tending his father-in-law's sheep (Exodus 3:1-2).

God called Deborah while she was judging Israel (Judges 4:4-5). God called Esther while she was serving as queen in the court of Ahasuerus (Esther 4:14). God called Amos while he was a shepherd in Tekoa (Amos 1:1). God called Isaiah while he was performing priestly duties in the Temple (Isaiah 6:1). And so on.

It appears, then, that one way to help discern our callings is to be engaged in some activity designed to promote the common good and strengthen the work of the church. In the matter of seeking our calling, our destination is sometimes not clear until after we have begun our journey.

The calling of Isaiah reminds us that God's call is one more expression of God's goodness. Why should God call a human to do something that God can call an angel to do? To call a human is a more thorough and excellent expression of God's love and grace. To call a frail human being to fulfill a divine purpose is a risk taken on God's part. It makes God's design vulnerable to human weakness and shortfall. Yet God is compelled by God's own love to take the risk. Our response to God's call should therefore ultimately be an expression of heartfelt thanksgiving.

My Calling

The light of dawn came as I lay in my bed one morning. I woke up earlier than usual and went back to sleep. I woke up again, but this time I did not stir. I could not stir. Though I seemed to be awake I could not move. I had a strange feeling of paralysis such as I never experienced before and have never experienced again. While lying there immobile, I heard words of announcement, "Call to preach. Call to preach. Kenneth. Kenneth." I then felt the unmistakable sensation of a finger pressing down upon my throat, causing me to gag, and shocking me out of my twilight state.

I woke up in a cold sweat and immediately looked over to my brother thinking that he was the one who touched my throat, but he was sound asleep in his bed.

Throughout the following week my morning experience haunted me and cast my soul into turmoil. I was in the grip of restless perplexity that drove me toward some unperceived resolution.

Finally, one day when I was completely alone in my parents' house, I sought an end to the anguish that was tearing at my soul.

How it dawned upon me to resolve my struggle the way that I did, I do not recall. But there in my loneliness I took my mother's Bible in hand, and posed a challenge to God.

"God, if you are calling me to preach, then allow me to open this Bible without fumbling to 2 Timothy 4:2 (Preach the word); and this is what I did. A powerful feeling came over me. I knew that this would happen. Furthermore, I knew that if I asked God to allow this a second time, this time with the page opening to John 21:15-17 (Feed my sheep, feed my lambs) it would be done. And it was done. A feeling of exhilaration mounted within me, but I wanted to be sure beyond a shadow of the doubt. "Just one more time, God," I asked. This time let the pages fall open to Matthew 28:19 (Go teach, baptize), a flip of the pages and there was the passage. It was done. I accepted my calling; and my soul was at peace.

This was twenty-five years ago. My experience of calling, of course, can be explained away by anyone who desires to explain it away; however, the significant point is that it can not be explained away by me, and I was the one who was there. The memory of my calling is, in fact, the core of my spiritual experience. It has proven both undeniable and unshakable.

I humbly offer my story for want of a better way to illustrate the experience of calling. May you also experience your calling in your own way, and may it prove to be an unshakable aspect of your spiritual life.

• *Chapter 8 Reflection Exercise* •

1. What form of activity or expression comes easily for you?

2. What is it that you love to do?

3. What are your natural gifts, graces, and talents?

4. What does your family or community affirm about you?

5. What already existing areas of service seem suitable for you?

6. What areas of service can you create if there appear to be none already suitable for you?

7. Have you discovered your calling?

8. What do you hear God calling you to do?

Here Am I!
• *Commitment* •

And I said, "Here am I; send me!"
— Isaiah 6:8

Yellow Jacket Tenacity

One of the churches I was assigned to at the beginning of my ministry was the smaller of a two-circuit charge deep in the heart of central Texas. Whenever it rained, the roads would be so badly washed out that it was impossible to get to the church. For this reason it was several weeks after I was assigned to the church that I was able to hold my first worship service there.

When the day finally came that I could penetrate deep enough into the backwoods to have a service there, I found an old paint-peeled structure of rotting wood that sort of leaned to one side. It was a humble little structure, to say the least.

I and members of the gradually arriving congregation entered and prepared for the start of church services. However, there was a problem.

Just over the pulpit area, hanging from a low overhead beam, was a nest of yellow-jacket wasps. I learned that they always built their nest in this same place between worship services. I also learned that day the congregation's routine procedure for getting rid of them.

After spying the wasps my chief steward went to his car, produced a plastic tube, and proceeded like an expert to siphon gasoline from his car. With jar of gasoline in hand he entered the church, walked up to the pulpit area, stood beneath the colony of wasps, and then doused the nest and ceiling areas with the fuel, killing the wasps on contact. Undoubtedly, this was a unique way of beginning worship that I never before witnessed, and have never witnessed again.

I observed, however, that despite my chief steward's obvious skill with this method of eradicating wasps, one or two of the critters would escape this petroleum onslaught, and fly around. And so, as I preached, I would have to keep one eye on the congregation and the other on the fugitive wasps.

Since then, I have always used those wasps as prime examples of commitment. Despite their constant experience of deadly dousing, those who survived would always go out and recruit more of their community so that by the time we gathered for worship again, there was a new colony of the little stingers in the very same place over the pulpit area.

That little church house in the backwoods now stands abandoned by the human congregation and taken over by the wasps; that is, if it is still standing at all. Persistence pays off, even for bugs. Oh, how I wish that our congregations could show the determination, the tenacity, and the commitment of those yellow jackets. Would we not flourish if it were so?

Maybe Isaiah would be a better example of commitment than our yellow jacket neighbors. His response to God's call through the commitment of himself is the climactic point in his testimony. As we explore his commitment, a few seldom-observed points are to be made by the context of Isaiah's decision.

Divine Playfulness

God has a wonderful sense of humor. Our spiritual perception is faulty if we have not yet realized this aspect of God's character. Witness God's dealing with Isaiah on the occasion of Isaiah's calling. God seems to ignore the presence of Isaiah while having a conversation with the heavenly host. Yes, I know, we have already cited this as an expression of God's holiness which makes God too high and far removed from the world to converse directly with a human being. But on the other hand, in light of the fact that God later speaks directly to Isaiah, we have to acknowledge that God at this point is also just playing around. It is almost as if God is saying to the angels, "Let's just ignore Isaiah and see what he does."

Isaiah stands therefore overhearing God's questioning of the seraphs about whom to commission and send, as if God were completely oblivious to Isaiah's presence in the room. What a laugh. How even more so comical that the all wise God would seek counsel from the seraphs as if God really needed their advice. Who is God kidding?

But there is a purpose to God's playfulness. God wishes to elicit from Isaiah a personal commitment for a quite serious task. Yet another paradox appears in this juxtaposition of humor and seriousness.

Isaiah's response appears tremendously brash when one considers that he was breaking into a conversation between the Almighty and the heavenly host, and brash it was. But this is what God intended.

How good humored God was to welcome Isaiah's intrusion into a session of the heavenly council. No doubt, the seraphs were accustomed to God's fun-loving ways and were not at all shocked by this encroachment upon their domain.

The idea that Isaiah had to announce his presence to God as if God did not know he was there, and the idea that God responded to Isaiah as if Isaiah was bailing God out and saving the day for the Lord is funny. One can imagine the smile on God's face as Isaiah responded to a question that, technically, no one asked him.

Isaiah's response to God's slyly given call was that of commitment. It was the yielding of his whole self to God's will for the purpose of fulfilling the call that Isaiah heard.

All That Matters

An interesting question occurs to us. Did Isaiah really know what he was doing by making such a commitment? How could he have known? Isaiah, who prophesied in Jerusalem, was called at the time when Israel (Ephraim) in the north was subjugated by Assyria, and Judah in the south had been reduced to no more than a minor province forced to pay taxes to the Assyrian giant.

Eight years after the call of Isaiah war broke out between Judah and an Israel-Syrian alliance (the Syro-Ephraimite War, 734–733 B.C.E.) (Isaiah 7:1-2). While Judah was defending itself, Edom also rose up and took the city of Elath from Judah's control (2 Kings 16:6). Against Isaiah's advice, King Ahaz of Judah appealed to Tiglath-pileser of Assyria for help (2 Kings 16:7-8). Also, in defiance of Isaiah, Ahaz, who became influenced by Assyrian religion, led the kingdom of Judah into idolatry (2 Kings 16:10-20). Later (715-705), after the death of Ahaz, Isaiah would warn King Hezekiah, son of Ahaz, against forming an alliance with Egypt against Assyria (Isaiah 20).

Hezekiah eventually went to war against Sennacherib of Assyria (2 Kings 18:13-17), and found himself and Judah under siege. Deliverance came, however, with the divinely arranged intervention of the army of Libnah (Isaiah 37:8) and King Tirhakah of Ethiopia (Isaiah 37:8-14).[9] All of this occurred in the ministry of Isaiah!

Furthermore, legend has it that Isaiah was killed when sawn in two by order of the evil King Manasseh of Judah. How could Isaiah possibly have known what he was getting into when he said, "Here am I"?

Yet, for Isaiah, it did not matter what he was getting into. The commitment of himself to his call was also an act of faith. And what is faith? It is the complete surrender of ourselves to the call of life in God. Come what may, Isaiah's life was given to God; and that is all that really mattered.

---

[9] See my *Afrocentric Sermons*, pp. 95–96.

Choice and Change

The transition from "woe is me" to "send me" was a quantum leap for Isaiah—a witness to the miracle of transformation in his being. First, he was so broken down in despair over his past that he could not move; but a few moments later, there he stood, ready for action.

Admittedly, the shift from paralysis to purpose may not happen as quickly for many of us. It may take time for God's transforming spirit to free us sufficiently from the weight of despair and despondency over past sin and shortfall so that we can serve God with enthusiasm and excitement. But this does not matter. What matters is that we yield to God's power and allow God to do the work of change regardless of how long it takes. The more we yield, however, the more quickly the process will go. We will find ourselves more and more energized to be what God wants and thus able to perform the service to which we are called. We will find ourselves more and more filled with the joy of spiritual freedom and surrender; and more and more ready to take on new tasks and fulfill them.

This, however, requires an act of letting go. There are those who hold on to their retrograde styles of life and self-defeating, self-destructive attitudes and habits for only one reason: they are familiar. We hold on to these patterns despite their detriment to us because they are comfortable. A way of life may be sucking us into a downwardly spiraling whirlpool, but we endure it because it is what we are accustomed to. For many, the only thing more frightening than a dismal future is change in the present. We simply do not know where we will end up if we make the commitment to a transformed life and new calling, and for some, this is reason enough to let things stay the way they are. Even more frightening to some than not knowing where they would end up is knowing that their present lives will change.

The truth of the matter is that those of us who hold on to self-destructive, self-defeating patterns of life still do not know where we will end up, but that doesn't matter because the present pattern of life is familiar. That pattern of life becomes a security blanket, even though the blanket is suffocating us.

We are called to make a commitment; a commitment to something and to Someone higher than we are; and this means letting go of past and present patterns and embracing a future with God.

Letting go is frightening to be sure; but then faith enters. Jesus told Simon Peter, "Launch out into the deep, and let down your nets for a catch" (Luke 5:4 author's paraphrase cf. KJV). In a sense, Jesus is still saying the same to us today. The deep is scary. Committing ourselves to going out into the deep is a staggering prospect for the deep represents the unknown future.

But it is out in the deep where we catch the substance of life, because the deep is not simply the unknown future, it is our future designed by God. Faith realizes this and is further strengthened when the catch happens.

So then where are love, opportunity, fulfillment, joy, peace, empowerment, meaning, direction, and other "big fish" caught? They are all caught out in the deep.

We are not speaking of reckless abandonment. We are not advocating a brainless rush to uncharted seas of adventure; nor are we speaking of ego-driven, undisciplined forays into whatever cause is available. We are speaking of a faithful response to the call of God.

And so here we are again, standing where Isaiah stood. No doubt the life of priest was a comfortable one for Isaiah. His aristocratic past still showed through in several of the things he wrote. But after his encounter with God, he knew that he could never again be comfortable. He could have tried, however, to be comfortable again in his old life. But it would have meant the death of new opportunity, the death of freedom, and the death of his soul. This is what a faithful response to God's call means for us also. But we have a choice, just as Isaiah did. It is nothing less than the choice of commitment.

The Leap of Faith

While visiting the San Diego Zoo one day, I took advantage of the opportunity to go on the guided tour. Our tour guide's procedure was to take us to various cages and open-air enclosures and then explain the traits and characteristics of the animals there.

We eventually came to one open-air enclosure containing a species of African gazelle. Only a small fence marked off the front of the enclosure.

In his usual manner, our tour guide proceeded to explain the traits and characteristics of this particular animal. Even though I cannot remember exactly what he said, I can reconstruct the essential lines of his speech.

"This animal" our tour guide explained, "has great leaping ability. In fact" the guide said, "this animal can easily leap out of its enclosure and escape to freedom. But it will not do that" he said, "because its enclosure is so constructed that the animal cannot see where it would land."

Our tour guide informed us that one thing this particular animal will not do is leap without being able to see where it would land. "This is why a cage is unnecessary for this animal," he said. "We call it a psychological barrier."

I came away from the gazelles with an insight. Freedom from that which binds us can be ours only if we are willing to make the leap of faith. But how often will we not make that leap simply because we cannot see where we might land?

Yes, empowerment can be ours, opportunity can be ours, fulfillment can be ours, joy can be ours, healing can be ours, peace can be ours, if only we are willing to make the commitment and take the leap! But we will not because we cannot see where we would land.

We, too, have our psychological barriers, or, perhaps we should say, spiritual barriers. The key to overcoming and discovering what lies beyond the barrier is the commitment that we make and the leap of faith that we take. Isaiah is our witness. He made the commitment. He took the leap of faith; and for him it meant power to be a prophet of God.

• *Chapter 9 Reflection Exercise* •

1. Name some rewards or "pay-offs" from commitments you have made.

2. Can you name any rewards or "pay-offs" from the particular commitment you made to be part of this study (or to read this book)? Write these down. If you are part of a study group, share them with the other members of your group.

3. What are two or three of the most important commitments you have made in your life?

4. How does faith help you to fulfill your most important commitments?

5. Are there any commitments that you feel summoned to but are hesitant to make? Please share them.

6. What should we pray for that would be helpful to you?

Go
• *Commission* •

And he said, "Go and say to this people:
  'Keep listening, but do not comprehend;
  keep looking, but do not understand.'
  Make the mind of this people dull,
    and stop their ears,
    and shut their eyes,
  so that they may not look with their eyes,
    and listen with their ears,
  and comprehend with their minds,
    and turn and be healed."
Then I said, "How long, O LORD?" And he said:
"Until cities lie waste without inhabitant,
    and houses without people,
    and the land is utterly desolate;
  until the LORD sends everyone far away,
    and vast is the emptiness in the midst of the land,
  Even if a tenth part remain in it,
    It will be burned again,
  like a terebinth or an oak
    whose stump remains standing
    when it is felled."
The holy seed is its stump.

— Isaiah 6:9-13

The Common Task

My day of fame had finally arrived—all two minutes of it. This was about how long the television station was going to give me and the other preachers who were there to render our talk before the camera.

The station had invited us to come for a taping of devotional messages which would be aired at sign-on time in the mornings. We were there from many different religious traditions. The person who went immediately before me was Hindu, and he spent half of his time chanting.

I wanted to give some poignant, insightful message that would have earthshaking effect; but what could I say in one or two minutes? It takes me that long to adjust my microphone on Sunday morning and even longer to give my sermon text and subject.

And so, I had to think hard about what I was going to say. I once heard someone state: to speak an hour requires no preparation at all, but to speak for a minute requires a lot.

I decided simply to tell a story and present a single lesson from it. I told my story of the gazelles who would not leap because they could not see where they would land, and pointed out how we are often like that.

And then it was over—just like that. Good-bye stardom, so long spotlight, arrivederci fame.

Several years have passed and so far I have not been asked to do any more tapings; and evidently, my message that day did not have earthshaking impact. However, I was told by a good friend and clergy colleague that she saw me on television one morning at about 5:00. Five o' clock in the morning?!! No wonder my message has not changed the world yet; no one was awake to hear it (other than my friend, of course).

Oh well, we must trudge on, and do our best to speak the words and perform the deeds that make for change.

All levity aside, this is what we are commissioned to do—to go out into the world, into our workplaces, our neighborhoods, our classrooms, our playgrounds, and our marketplaces to change things for the better.

Although Isaiah the prophet is our example, one does not have to be a prophet to be commissioned for the work of transforming society. Ours is a common calling for the good of humankind. True, some among us are called and commissioned for specialized works and services. They serve to bring focus and leadership to the common task of social transformation to which we are all called.

They serve also as reminders of an important truth, namely, that vital spirituality must be translated into social ministry. Mistaken is the notion that spiritual life and development is solely a private, inner matter that has only to do with a person's relationship to God. Indeed, true spirituality also involves our relationship with our fellow human beings and our response to their needs.

As we explore Isaiah's commission, we must be mindful that he was sent not only to challenge spiritual failure, but also social failure. As far as the prophet was concerned, there was no distinction between the two kinds of failure. The unfaithful failed God because they failed their fellow human beings, and they failed their fellow human beings because they failed God. The judgment the people faced was, therefore, for a single act of apostasy that involves falling away from both spiritual and social faithfulness. A closer look at Isaiah's experience of commissioning helps us to see the full scope of our responsibility.

Judgment and Restoration

The prophet is more a broadcaster than a forecaster. Prophecy is not so much a crystal ball as it is a magnifying glass. The purpose of prophetic ministry is to make God's word and will clear to the people of the land.

We see this especially in the case of Isaiah. Isaiah was commissioned or sent with a message of judgment upon the people of Judah for refusing to see and hear God's truth so that they might be healed.

Judgment in God's message to Isaiah took three basic forms: judgment upon the people themselves (verses 9-8), judgment upon the land (verse 11), and judgment upon the identity and existence of Judah as a nation (verses 12-13). The first judgment meant sickness and death; the second, ruin; and the third, exile.

The reasons for judgment appear in the breadth of Isaiah's message. Judgment was for failure to cleanse the nation of pagan religious influences and idolatry (Isaiah 2:5-8; 17:7-11), failure to refrain from military alliances with pagan nations (Isaiah 30:1-17; 31:1-3), and failure to do justice (Isaiah 1:17).

Israel, Assyria, Egypt, Ethiopia, Babylon, Philistia, Moab, Edom, and other nations also received the pronouncement of judgment in the message of Isaiah for their disobedience, arrogance, and cruelty.

The message of Isaiah was not all doom and gloom, however. Despite judgment there was the promise of restoration and healing for Judah (Isaiah 29:1-8) and conversion and salvation for such nations as Ethiopia, Egypt, and Assyria (Isaiah 18:7; 19:23-25). The message of Isaiah was a summons to both spiritual and social wholeness.

Divine Urgency

All things considered, it is startling that God spoke directly to Isaiah this time. No seraph delivered the content of God's message to the prophet. There was no further observance of the protocol of interaction between the Divine and the human. Divine playfulness was laid aside. Suddenly God spoke directly to the prophet; and this was an event of extraordinary significance. Urgency was the factor that caused this divinely initiated breach in protocol. Urgency is underscored as God spoke to Isaiah once, and even a second time, in response to Isaiah's question "how long?" (verse 11).

The message of judgment and restoration was urgently important to God in Isaiah's day; too urgent and too important to mediate through angels. The urgency and importance of God's message remains today, because now, as in Isaiah's day, God cares for the people.

God says in effect, "Judgment is the consequence of false worship. Judgment is the consequence of disobedience and injustice; but repentance and obedience are also the way to healing and restoration, to salvation."

> "Come now, let us argue it out,
>   says the LORD:
> though your sins are like scarlet,
>   they shall be like snow;
> though they are red like crimson,
>   they shall become like wool."
>   — Isaiah 1:18

Prophetic Courage

In recent years we have been witnesses to extraordinary events and upheavals on the geo-political landscape. We have seen the collapse of the Soviet Union, the dissolution of Yugoslavia, the dismantling of the Berlin Wall, the end of South African apartheid, and the social uprising in the City of Los Angeles to name only a few.

These are times of swift transition and instability in the social-political sphere. These are also times of spiritual chaos and moral breakdown; and this makes for a volatile combination in the global game room.

We still need prophets to summon us back to the spiritual roots of wholeness and peace. We still need broadcasters of God's word and magnifiers of God's truth, so that we will understand and turn and be healed.

However, not all are called and commissioned to be prophets. Yet this does not leave the rest of us without a task. All of us are called and commissioned to demonstrate prophetic courage. What does this mean?

Prophetic courage is holding up the standards of justice for all people, especially the historically oppressed and disenfranchised. It is challenging all falsehoods and half-truths whether they are spoken in private or in the public forum. It is proclaiming the need for moral principles and moral education. It is defending against the erosion of spirituality in life. It is working for the creation of goodwill in our communities and across cultural lines. It is promoting the ideals of goodness and kindness.

Yes, it is true that in all these areas there is debate about what all of this means. It looks as if we shall continue to debate for a long time. However, our commitment requires us to believe that out of the bubbling ferment of debate, God is forging a consensus that will prevail to bring salvation to the people.

Not all are called and commissioned to be prophets, but we all have spiritual vocations assigned to us by God. We should pursue these vocations with the determination and tenacity of an Isaiah or Deborah.

And so the day is upon us. We can no longer afford to hide our heads under the cover of complacency. We are the people of God, and we must rise to the challenge of prophetic engagement with our society.

Streets of Fire

The four-mile thoroughfare to my church was a corridor of fire in the summer of 1992. The city of Los Angeles had exploded into a rage over the outcome of an intensely watched trial. Years of anger and frustration poured out into the streets and burst into chaos.

I felt I needed to get to the church and respond to the situation from there; I at least needed to know what was happening in the neighborhood around the church.

Once out in the streets I wondered if coming out was a mistake. Driving a direct route became impossible. My route was cut off by plumes of fire and smoke. The old familiar liquor stores and family markets that dotted the street were ablaze. Abandoned vehicles and rioting people contributed to an apocalyptic scene.

I was forced to take several detours on my way to the church. It was taking me three times the usual driving time to get there, but I was out now and I thought that I may as well continue. Sirens screamed in the distance, but no rescue vehicles were visible, and ravaging fire met no resistance.

I approached the church from the south; I had completely abandoned my usual western route. A car coming out of the east cut close to my front end while turning at the intersection; its wide-eyed driver shouted something to me, but I thought it best to drive on.

I was thankful that the church building and surrounding homes were unharmed; but the supermarket up the street and nearby liquor stores were consumed in flame.

After arriving at the church, I found it empty. Satisfying myself that the church was in no danger and people in their homes were going to stay inside, I decided it was best that I head back home.

The return was just as torturous as the coming. An unnerving incident on the return trip was the fright of hearing gunshots within feet of my car as I passed a blighted corner. My body automatically scrunched down in my seat as the explosive sounds seemed to occur just outside my sideview window.

I finally made it back home, but in the days that followed I was back at the church working in conjunction with social service agencies to bring help and relief to a hurting community. Hundreds, perhaps one or two thousand, came to the church with need for food and supplies. Help poured in from grocery store chains, warehouses, private donors, and volunteers. These were days of turmoil and uncertainty. Even the church had to struggle with what it meant to be the church in those days when we had to open our doors to the hungry, displaced, and the strange.

These were also the days of clamoring voices—voices of protest, voices of anger, voices of anguish, voices of truth, voices of deception, and voices of peace; but in the midst of these voices were also the voices of the prophets—the Isaiahs, the Deborahs, the Huldahs, the Jeremiahs, the Ezekiels, the Miriams, the Daniels, the Amoses, the Zechariahs—people who had been called and commissioned to speak to the troubled times.

Now that the fires have died down, so have some of the clamoring voices; but the prophets are still speaking, just as they were before things exploded, and they are still calling us to obedience, truth, and justice lest the fires rage again.

Is anyone listening? Is anyone listening?!

Isaiah would find these times hauntingly familiar, but he would not be daunted in challenging us to translate our spirituality into acts of social healing.

• *Chapter 10 Reflection Exercise* •

1. What would you say are the critical social needs of your community?

2. What would you say are the most critical spiritual needs of your community?

3. If your church or faith community had unlimited resources, what type of ministries would you recommend for the good of the community?

4. Brainstorm about how your dreams for social ministry and Christian service can be adapted to the realities of your present church situation.

5. Think about how the gifts, talents, and abilities that you have identified in yourself can be used in ministry to your community. Share these with your group.

6. What new possibilities do you see for the work of your church in your community? Please share them.

Study Leader's Guide
• *Six-Part Study Series* •

This resource easily lends itself to a ten-part study series; however, already busy people might prefer to commit to a shorter period of time. Therefore, this leader's guide is designed for a six-part study with sessions scheduled for once a week. A study leader may want to poll potential participants about the kind of scheduling that would be most appealing.

The format offered here should be considered flexible in all cases and dispensable in some cases. It is impossible to provide a teaching plan that would anticipate the many variations in setting, class size, leadership skill, language, culture, and needs that will be brought to this study. This guide may prove to be no more than a place to begin.

Nevertheless, the effort here is to show at least one way this book can be a resource for persons seeking to deepen their understanding of spiritual life.

Basic Recommendations

Each member of the study session should obtain a copy of *I Saw the Lord* and read the chapters to be discussed in each session prior to the session. Participants may also read the questions or discussion starters at the end of each chapter and begin thinking about how they might respond.

As study leader, you may want to do some background study of the Book of Isaiah to enrich your leadership of the sessions. A great variety of material is available. The following books are recommended:

Christopher R. Seitz, *Isaiah 1-39, Interpretation: A Bible Commentary for Teaching and Preaching* (Louisville: John Knox Press, 1993).

Herbert M. Wolf, *Interpreting Isaiah: The Suffering and Glory of the Messiah* (Grand Rapids: Zondervan Publishing House, 1985).

A Basic Format for All Sessions

Length of sessions: 1-1/2 hours.
Size of class: 10–25 people.
Format:

1. Leader's Remarks (10 minutes)
2. Leader asks participants to respond to reflection exercises at end of assigned chapters (15 minutes). Note: In cases where two chapters are assigned to a session, a few items from each reflection exercise should be selected. Participants should be assigned no more than six or seven reflection items.
3. Leader asks participants to form groups of three to five people to share among themselves responses to reflection exercises (20 minutes).
4. Leader calls group back together and asks a volunteer from each group to share general observations or discoveries from his or her group (15 minutes).
5. Leader allows for any further questions, comments, or discoveries from the total group (10 minutes).
6. Leader allows time to consider requests for special prayer (15 minutes).
7. Leader assigns chapters in *I Saw the Lord* to be read for next session.
8. Note: Adjust session time to allow for evaluation at the end of session six.

Session Suggestions for Study Leaders

Session One

1. Leader's Remarks: Share what you have learned from your outside readings about the reigns of Uzziah and Ahaz. Offer your own opinion about the significance of Uzziah's death to Isaiah.
2. Assign chapters 2 and 3 for next session.

Session Two
1. Leader's remarks: Share what you have learned from outside readings about the role and importance of Isaiah in the teachings of Jesus and the message of other New Testament personalities. Make general comments about the relationship of the Old Testament to the New Testament.
2. Assign chapters 4 and 5 for next session.

Session Three
1. Leader's remarks: Share what you have learned from your reading about the setting of Isaiah's vision in the temple and about the seraphs. Offer your insights about the role and importance of sound, music, color, and feeling in worship.
2. Assign chapters 6 and 7 for next session.

Session Four
1. Leader's remarks: Share what you have learned from your readings about the political conflict in Judah during the time of Isaiah and the reigns of Ahaz and Hezekiah.
2. Assign chapters 8 and 9 for next session.

Session Five
1. Leader's remarks: share what you have learned about the purpose of Isaiah's ministry and about the content of his general message in chapters 1-39.
2. Assign chapter 10 for next session.
3. Make preparation to evaluate the study sessions and study book at the end of the final session.

Session Six
1. Leader's remarks: Share what you have learned about the importance of social justice in the preaching of Isaiah.
2. Lead the group in evaluation of study sessions and study book. See page 110 for a suggested evaluation exercise.

A Suggested Evaluation Exercise

Conduct the evaluation exercise during the last forty-five minutes of the final session. Ask each member of the study group to do the following:

1. Reflect upon each item listed below and consider: "In what way(s) was this particular part of the study helpful? What could have been done to make this particular part more helpful? Jot down brief responses as you apply these questions to each item below (twelve minutes).

    -   Leader's remarks
    -   Reflection exercises
    -   Small group sharing
    -   Study sessions
    -   Content of *I Saw the Lord*

2. Briefly write down any general thoughts or feelings that you have about this six-week study experience (three minutes).

3. Return to your small group and take turns briefly sharing what you have written (fifteen minutes).

4. Return to general assembly and by means of a group spokesperson give a quick overview of your small group discussion. Ask for a volunteer to record observations that might be helpful for future sessions (fifteen minutes).

5. Close in a manner appropriate to your group. Forward relevant evaluative comments to *I Saw the Lord*, Upper Room Books, P.O. Box 189, Nashville, TN 37202-0189.

· *Cover Art Interpretation* ·

by Sheila R. Williams

A cocoon of vivid, vibrant, living cover enveloped my being as I absorbed the reflection of the author. These passionate, provoking meditations from the book of Isaiah gave birth to the polychromatic handcrafted paper illustration titled *Freedom*. Inspired by the multiplicities of Pan African artistic tradition, *Freedom* through a freehand style captures the perfect and imperfect intricacies of the spiritual sojourn. As you move through *Freedom*, experience the natural and mechanical message in each color and image as a road map leading you to wholeness.

- LIGHT: Circle. God. Nkyinkyim-Adinkra border espousing African value: changing oneself. Truth. (I saw the Lord.)

- YELLOW/GOLD: Six wings. Seraphim. Service and love. (The whole earth is full of God's glory.)

- BROWN/BURNT ORANGE: Coal. Moving anger. (Guilt removed)

- GREEN: Tree of Life. Healing. (Sins forgiven)

- BLUE: Creation. Sensitivity. Spirit connection. (Who will go for us?)

- PURPLE: Isaiah. Deeper connection to the spirit. (Send me.)

- RED: Seed. Passion. Hope. Holy seed. (This is when we know that we have seen the Lord.)

• *About the Author* •

Kenneth L. Waters Sr. is the pastor of the Vermont Square United Methodist Church of Los Angeles and chief spiritual director of the Los Angeles Inner City Walk to Emmaus Community. He holds degrees from Paul Quinn College, Waco, Texas and Perkins School of Theology, Southern Methodist University, Dallas, Texas. He is a candidate for the Ph.D. in New Testament at Fuller Theological Seminary, Pasadena, California.

Reverend Waters enjoys reading, writing, science fiction movies, and weight lifting. He is married to Justine Bell Waters, and they have five sons.